Impact of COVID-19 on Rural India

Impact of COVID-19 on Rural India

Editor

Dr. Rajesh Kumar Sinha

KALPAZ

First Published, 2020

Published by

Kalpaz Publications
C-30, Satyawati Nagar,
Delhi – 110052
Ph.: 011-47034999, 9811692060
www.kalpazpublications.com
E-mail: kalpaz@hotmail.com

Printed at: Gyan Press, Delhi

Cataloging in Publication Data—DK
Courtesy: D.K. Agencies (P) Ltd. <docinfo@dkagencies.com>

Impact of COVID-19 on rural India / editor, Dr. Rajesh Kumar Sinha.
pages cm
Contributed articles.
ISBN 9789353242855 (HB)

1. COVID-19 (Disease)—Economic aspects—India. 2. COVID-19 (Disease)—Social aspects—India. 3. India—Rural conditions. I. Sinha, Rajesh Kumar, editor.

LCC RA644.C67I47 2020 | DDC 616.2414 23

Contents

Preface and Acknowledgement 7
List of Contributors 9

1. COVID-19 in Rural India: An Introduction 13
   — Dr. Rajesh Kumar Sinha
2. Impact of COVID-19 on Rural Migrants in India 29
   — Dr. Sakshi Sahni, Dr. Rawal Singh Aulakh
3. Impact of COVID 19 on Single Women in Rural India 41
   — Mr. Anthony Chettri, Ms. Bedadyuti Jha
4. Impact of COVID-19 on Indian Migrant Workers in the Gulf Countries 51
   — Dr. Trilok Chandan Goud
5. Role Played by Self Help Groups in Combating COVID-19 in Odisha 63
   — Dr. Biswa Mohana Jena, Dr. Binita Nanda
6. Role of Pachayats amidst COVID-19: Study of Sonitpur District of Assam 73
   — Mr. Mohan Pathak
7. Role of Panchayats in Managing COVID-19 in Rural Areas 85
   — Ms. Chitra Chandra
8. Impact of COVID-19 on Rural Wage Employment: Analysis of MGNREGA 95
   — Dr. Rajesh Kumar Sinha
9. Impact of COVID-19 on Rural Economy of India 103
   — Ms. Anindita Mukherjee
10. Impact of Covid -19 on Handicraft Clusters in India 115
    — Ms. Jasmeet Kaur

11. Impact of COVID-19 on Rural Self Help Groups (SHGs) 125
— Dr. Shafia Wani

12. Impact of COVID-19 on Rural Livelihoods: A Sociological Study of Telangana 133
— Mr. Sreeramulu Gosikonda

13. Impact of COVID-19 on Rural Education in India 145
— Dr. Rajeev Bansal

14. Impact of COVID-19 on Rural Society of Sikkim 159
— Ms. Jashi M. Gurung

15. MGNREGA and Social Audit amidst COVID-19 169
— Dr. Vikas Jha

Index 177

Preface and Acknowledgement

COVID-19/is/a disease/caused by a new strain of Coronavirus. 'CO' stands for corona, 'VI' for virus, and 'D' for disease. COVID-19 has impacted the entire world and also India like never before. Though started as urban menace, the disease has now spread to rural areas and the proportion of affected persons in rural areas is increasing continuously. Impact of Rural India has been felt more as loss of urban livelihoods has also impacted remittance to rural areas from migrant labours working in urban areas. Inadequate health facilities, poor internet connectivity and lack of media attention to rural areas have further made rural community more vulnerable. Disturbance of agricultural operations due to non-availability of inputs, labour and marketing avenues have given a serious jolt to agricultural based rural economy.

Government of India, State Governments and local authorities including Panchayats have responded to the challenge and have raised awareness of rural community, provided financial assistance, food grains, safety gears, quarantine facilities in collaboration with Self-Help Groups (SHGs) and Civil Society Organisations (CSOs). However, there is much to be done to mitigate sufferings of rural community.

Present book deals with impact of COVID-19 on various dimensions of rural India: economy, local-self governance, self-help groups, wage employment, gulf-migrants, vulnerable communities such as single women, rural livelihoods, rural education, rural society, social audit etc. Chapters of this book, based on analytical and empirical studies, analyse challenges faced by these sectors, response of government and non-government institutions and recommend measures for managing COVID-19 and such disasters in future more effectively. This book will be highly useful for scholars of rural development, media persons, policy makers and civil society organisations.

I express my gratitude to all chapter authors, who are experienced researchers, academicians and development practitioners, for taking time out from their busy schedule to contribute chapters at a relatively short notice. I would also like to thank my present and ex-colleagues for their inputs and suggestions on the draft of this book. My special thanks to Dr. Vinay Sahasrabuddhe, Dr. Atanu Mohapatra, Dr. Rakesh Sinha, Shri N.N. Sinha for their constant inspiration and guidance. Last but not the least, I thank my family members, my wife and daughter for their constant cooperation and support.

Dr. Rajesh Kumar Sinha
September, 2020
Hyderabad

List of Contributors

Dr. Sakshi Sahni is an Assistant Professor in Guru Ram Das School of Planning, Guru Nanak Dev University, Amritsar. She has done her B.Tech (Urban and Regional Planning) from Guru Nanak Dev University, Amritsar and Master of Infrastructure Planning from CEPT Univeristy, Ahmedabad. She has 8 years of teaching experience and 10 years of research work.

Dr. Rawal Singh Aulakh is an Assistant Professor in Department of Architecture, Guru Nanak Dev University, Amritsar, Punjab. He has done Masters in Urban Planning from Guru Ram Das School of Planning, Guru Nanak Dev University, Amritsar and Ph.D. in Architecture on 'Evolution of Golden Temple, Amritsar'. He has 10 years of teaching experience.

Mr. Anthony Chettri is working with Indo Global Social Service Society (IGSSS) as Lead – Programme Development, Support and Management and is also pursuing his Ph.D. in Social Work from Amity University, Noida. He is a qualified social worker with over 19 years of experience. He started his career as a field-level worker in a grassroots organisation and then moved to become a Lecturer followed by working in different national and international NGOs in India.

Ms. Bedadyuti Jha is working with Indo Global Social Service Society (IGSSS) as Research Officer. She is a development professional with 6 years of experience in the areas of gender,health, and labour. She has a Master's Degree in Women's Studies from TISS, Mumbai

Dr. Trilok Chandan Goud is Post Doctoral Research Fellow in Department of Sociology, University of Hyderabad. He holds received his PhD from the UGC Center for the Study of Indian Diaspora, University of Hyderabad, India. His research areas include study of migration and diaspora. His Post Doctoral research is on Social Networks and Transnational Migration. He has presented papers in national and international conferences and contributed papers to journals.

Dr. Biswa Mohana Jena is currently Head, Department Of Commerce in Netaji Subhas Chandra Bose College, Sambalpur. He has teaching experience of 10 years with research interests in Auditing, Financial accounting, Cost accounting, Management accounting, Business statistics, Financial management etc. He has published 60 research papers in international journal authored books like Management Accounting, Financial Management, Auditing and Corporate governance, Business law and Fundamentals of Entrepreneurship.

Dr. Binita Nanda is currently working as a Faculty at JKBK Govt. College. She holds Ph.D degree in Commerce. Dr. Nanda has published research articles in various national and international UGC approved journals.

Mr. Mohan Pathak is a Research Scholar in the Department of Political Science, Rajiv Gandhi University, Arunachal Pradesh. He is presently doing M.Phil on "Electoral Participation of Tea Tribes of Assam: A study of Monabari Tea Garden under Biswanath District". He has presented research papers in various international and national seminars and conferences and has published 6 papers in international and national journals and ISBN books. His areas of interest are Electoral politics, Party Politics, Women in Politics, Grassroots democracy and Indian Constitution.

Ms. Chitra Chandra is currently working as Master Trainer with Society for Training and Research on Panchayats & Rural Development (STARPARD), Panchayats & Rural Development Department, Government of West Bengal. She holds Masters in Rural Development and Management and has 12 yrs of experience in capacity building of Elected Representatives and Functionaries of the Panchayti Raj Institutions. Areas of her domain expertise include Acts & Rules related to Functioning of Gram Panchayats, Financial Management of Gram Panchayats, Public Health, Gram Panchayat Development Plan, Women and Child Development.

Dr. Rajesh Kumar Sinha is working as Assistant Professor with the National Institute of Rural Development and Panchayati Raj (NIRD&PR), Hyderabad. He holds Ph.D. degree from JNU, New Delhi with UGC- Senior Research Fellowship in Public Administration. His research interests lie in rural local governance, rural development, social audit, social accountability, capacity building and international relations. He has worked with UNDP, Union Ministry of Panchayati Raj, PRIA, IDRF and Sewa International in the past. Dr. Sinha has authored and edited several books and contributed articles to edited books and reputed journals on various topics related to rural development and Panchayati Raj.

Ms. Anindita Mukherjee is currently working as Decentralized Planning Facilitation Coordinator with STARPARD, Panchayat & Rural Development Department, West Bengal. She holds Master Degree in Economics Rabindra Bharati University, Kolkata and is UGC NET qualified. She has more than 15 years of experience working as Lecturer and Decentralized Planning Facilitation Coordinator at the district and State level.

Ms. Jasmeet Kaur is a Research Scholar at the Mittal School of Business, Lovely Professional University, Phagwara, Punjab. She has completed her MBA in Retail Management from Amity University, ADDOE, Noida and PG Diploma in Fashion Retail Management from National Institute of Fashion Technology (NIFT), Delhi. Her professional experience includes full time and part time Lecturer positions at Y.W.C.A, Raffles Millennial International, Delhi and New Delhi YMCA. Her area of research includes Fashion marketing, Sustainable Fashion and Slow Fashion.

Dr. Shafia Wani is a Faculty at Jammu and Kashmir Institute of Management Public Administration and Rural Development (IMPARD). She is a trainer and development professional with an experience of more than 16 years with international NGOs and state agencies in social work and rural development, rights based and emergency programmes in Kashmir. She holds Ph.D. degree from University of Kashmir and has contributed research articles in national and international journals.

Mr. Sreeramulu Gosikonda is currently working as a Lecturer in Sociology at the Department of Agricultural Science and Rural Development in Loyola Academy Degree & PG College, Alwal, Secunderabad. He has submitted his Ph. D. (Sociology) thesis to University of Hyderabad. His areas of research include Sociology of Education, Rural Sociology, Urban Sociology, Political Sociology, Research Methods and Rural Development.

Dr. Rajeev Bansal is Deputy Director (Research) in the Faculty of Rural Development under the H.P. Institute of Public Administration, Fairlawn, Shimla and former Director, Social Audit Unit, Himachal Pradesh. He holds a Ph.D. on Social Audit from Rural Development Department, Gandhigram Rural University, Tamil Nadu. His area of training and research include Rural Development, Panchayati Raj, Development Administration, Transparency & Accountability, Management Development, Administrative Reforms, Research Methodology, Participatory Training, Gender Mainstreaming and

Process Documentation. He has published many studies and reports for government, articles in national and international journals.

Ms. Jashi M. Gurung is M.Phil. Scholar in the Department of Sociology, Sikkim University. She is NET and SLET qualified. Presently she conducting research on 'Elopement based marriage in Sikkim'. Her area of interest are Family, Marriage and Kinship.

Dr. Vikas Jha is Director, Good Rural Governance, Sehgal Foundation. He has a PhD from JNU, New Delhi and holds a postgraduate diploma in Policy Studies from the University of London. He has eighteen years of professional experience in the development sector and field experience in India, Brazil, South Africa, South East Asia, and South Asia on issues of social accountability and decentralised governance.

Chapter - 1

COVID-19 in Rural India: An Introduction

— Dr. Rajesh Kumar Sinha

COVID-19

As per World Health Organization (WHO), COVID-19/is/a disease/caused by a new strain of Coronavirus. 'CO' stands for corona, 'VI' for virus, and 'D' for disease. Formerly, this disease was referred to as '2019 novel coronavirus' or '2019-nCoV' (WHO, 2020a). The COVID-19 virus is a new virus linked to the same family of viruses as Severe Acute Respiratory Syndrome (SARS) and some types of common cold. Older people and people with chronic medical conditions, /such as diabetes and heart disease, /appear to be more at risk of developing severe symptoms, if infected. The disease spreads primarily through contact with an infected person when they cough or sneeze and virus gets released with tiny droplets. It also spreads when a person touches a surface or an object that has the virus on it, then touches her/his eyes, nose, or mouth. Therefore, it is recommended worldwide that one can protect oneself by washing hands frequently, avoiding touching face, and avoiding close contact (1 meter or 3 feet) with people who are unwell. The most common symptoms of COVID-19 are fever, tiredness, and dry cough. Some patients may have aches and pains, nasal congestion, runny nose, sore throat or diarrhoea. These symptoms are usually mild and begin gradually. The WHO has reported that there is no currently available vaccine for COVID-19 and that several research institutes and laboratories in different countries are at various stages of developing vaccine. However, many of the symptoms can be treated and getting early care from a healthcare provider can make the disease less dangerous. It is pandemic and therefore it can last for a longer time though there are measures to slow down the spread. As per the WHO directions, public health measures are critical to slow the spread of illnesses. Public health measures are everyday preventive actions that include: staying home when sick; covering mouth and nose with flexed elbow or tissue when coughing or sneezing etc. and dispose of used tissue immediately; washing hands often with soap and water or alcohol based sanitizers; and sanitizing frequently touched surfaces and objects etc. (WHO, 2020b).

COVID-19 in India

India's response to COVID-19 has been pre-emptive, pro-active and graded. India had already put in place a comprehensive response system at its borders much before WHO declared it as a public health emergency of international concern on 30th January, 2020. Thermal screening of incoming international passengers from China and Hong Kong was started on 18th January, 2020, much before the first case of Corona Virus was detected in India on 30th January. Government of India took a number of proactive measures, such as travel restrictions, adding more countries and airports for screening, suspension of visas and self quarantine measures to effectively contain, prevent and manage the spread of the disease (Ministry of Information and Broadcasting, 2020). However, despite all these precautionary measures, with international travellers Corona Virus also entered into India and slowly started spreading to all over the country. Government of India declared it a national disaster and invoked provisions of National Disaster Management Act, 2005 and also announced to provide assistance under Disaster Response Fund. Further, the Government of India adopted a complete lockdown from 23rd March to 14th April 2020 which was extended three times with some progressive relaxations, first up to 3rd May, second up to 17th May and third up to 31st May 2020. Thereafter process of gradual unlock started with empowerment of State Governments and local authorities to take measures as per local situations to contain the disease. The Epidemic Diseases (Amendment) Ordinance was promulgated on 22nd April, 2020 amending the provisions of the Epidemic Diseases Act, 1897. These measures have not only slowed down the spread of the disease but also provided ample time to Central, State and local administration to prepare to deal with the situation. However, cases kept only slowly increasing all over the country. According to the union Ministry of Health and Family Welfare, the total cumulative number of COVID-29 cases in the country stands at 34,63,972 with total 7,52,424 active cases, total 26,48,998 discharged cases and total 62,550 cases of death due to COVID-19 as on (source: https://www.mygov.in/covid-19/).

COVID-19 in Rural India

Although COVID-19 started and remained concentrated in urban India for some time, with reverse migrations and relaxations in movements after start of unlock, it has also spread to rural India. Inadequate awareness due to low literacy and lack of media exposure, limited supply of clean water, low levels of nutrition, and ill-equipped and insufficient public health centres and district hospitals has made rural India vulnerable (Mitra, 2020). The union Ministry of Health and Family Welfare study points out that there is a 12 percent deficiency of Primary Health Centers (PHC) and 50 percent of Community Health Centers (CHC) across Rural India (Nair, 2020). Out of the 178,671,105 rural households, 77 percent are waiting to get a household connection (Sengupta, 2020). Proportion of rural population till the month of May 2020 continued to be far less in comparison to urban areas. In Maharashtra 27 municipal corporations contributed about 94 percent of the cases. Villages and small towns put together accounted for only six percent. Similarly, in Karnataka, all cities and towns contributed 92 percent of the State's cases, with rural areas showing a share of 8 percent. (Shylendra, 2020). However, towards after May 2020, many cases beyond municipal boundaries all over the country have been reported and the percentage of rural people testing corona positive is increasing fast. By the middle of August, 2020 increased spread to rural areas have been noticed as serious threat. The virus has spread to about 711 of 739 districts, including 100 of the country's poorest rural areas. Several districts in nine major states — Bihar, Madhya Pradesh, Telangana, Jharkhand, Uttar Pradesh, Maharashtra, West Bengal, Odisha and Gujarat, all of which have sizable rural populations, are highly vulnerable to new infections, according to a Lancet study (Pradhan, 2020). On August 10, 2020, rural and semi-urban centres accounted for 47% of fresh infections, or almost double their share as compared to a month ago. Fresh infections in semi-urban regions rose faster than those in rural areas, from 13.3% of the country's total infection a month ago to 27.3% on August 10. The urban share of new infections during this period fell from 75% to 53%. In terms of new deaths, rural areas are growing faster than any other areas. While the share of urban areas in fresh daily deaths fell to 69.7% on August 10, from 84.2% a month ago, that for semi-urban areas rose to 18.5% from 10.1%. The share of rural areas, however, more than doubled to 11.8% from 5.7% earlier. In terms of total infections, not just fresh infections, rural and semi-urban regions now account for over a one-third of total cases. They accounted for a 20% share a month back. By the month-end, rural and semi-urban regions may account for nearly half of total infections (Gera, 2020).

Impact of COVID-19 on Rural India

Impact of the COVID-19 has been felt on every aspects of rural life. A significant proportion of rural household income comes from migrant labour and also daily wage labour in nearby areas which got completely disturbed for at least two months during the lockdown. According to a study conducted in a tribal village of Dahod and a non-tribal village of Surendranagar of Gujarat in the year 2019, on an average, migration helped households earn annually Rs. 1.34 lakh in the tribal village and Rs. 1.68 lakh in the non-tribal village. This constituted about 69 percent and 38 percent of the total income of the households in these two villages, respectively (Shylendra, 2020). Part of perishable items from rural areas such as milk, vegetables, fruits, meat products and eggs got spoilt or sold cheaply due to lower off-take and closure of local markets during the lockdown leading to heavy losses to small and marginal farmers. Further, farmers could not get enough agricultural labour to harvest their Rabi crop which they were getting earlier as many migrant labours working in urban areas used to shift to rural areas during peak agricultural season. This situation led to delay in harvesting and also increased the cost due to scarcity of labour. Lack of availability of seeds, fertilizer, and farm machinery during the lockdown has delayed sowing of next crop (Mitra, 2020). Disruption of collection and sale of non-timber forest produces during the lockdown has badly affected tribal communities and forest dwellers (Bhavani, 2020). Complete shutdown of exports have negatively impacted agricultural exports and associated farmers. Cottage and small industries and businesses based in rural areas have piled up inventories and as a result have retrenched employees leading to increase in unemployment in rural areas. Uncertain future has also stalled their expansion plans (Khan, 2020). Those operating shared transports in rural areas such as auto, jeep etc. have lost their livelihoods during the lockdown and have lesser income even now as people are avoiding these shared transport facilities as much as possible. A study conducted by Amrita University on impact of COVID-19 on households of SHGs in Kerala found that about 77% of the principal income generators were reported to have stopped working during the lockdown (although they did not lose their job); an additional 12% have also stopped working but have lost their job. About 10% are still working as usual (Amrita News Service, 2020). The dearth of employment avenues in rural areas has increased the number of people who are taking up petty trade and manual labour under Mahatma Gandhi National Employment Guarantee Act (MGNREGA). There have been reports of private school teachers, skilled industrial workers and other educated persons who were earlier employed in organized or unorganized private sector demanding job under MGNREGA to get some income to survive the crisis. Education in rural areas has suffered due to inadequate internet connectivity, lesser usage smart phones, irregular electricity supply and lack of initiatives by teachers of government schools in rural areas. There have been no or negligible online classes unlike urban areas where this has become the new normal. Nair (2020) argues that the connectivity issues create problems for States in digitalizing education and inadequate connectivity has also affected in delivering proper information to people in rural areas. Poor, homeless, destitute, single women, elderly persons without caretakers have been particularly vulnerable as they remained dependent on government's social assistance or charity from civil society organisations. A survey of 5,162 households across 47 districts in 12 states between April 28 and May 2, 2020 jointly conducted by PRADAN, Action for Social Advancement, BAIF, Transform Rural India Foundation, Grameen Sahara, SAATHI-UP and The Aga Khan Rural Support Programme (India) found that 68 percent had reduced food items in their meals, 50 percent had reduced the number of times they were eating in a day and 24 percent of them had borrowed food grain.

Governmental and Non-Governmental Responses

Government of India, State Governments and Panchayati Raj Institutions (PRIs) took note of these challenges faced by villagers and reverse migrants in rural areas and responded to their needs. Government of India announced an assistance of Rs.1.70 lakh crore as Prime Minister's Garib Kalyan Package on 26th March, 2020 aimed at providing immediate relief to poor and vulnerable, including provision of five kg. wheat/ rice per person per month and one kg. pulses free per households for three months; cash transfers of Rs.500 per month for the three months in Jan Dhan Yojana accounts of 20 crore women; ex-gratia of Rs.1000 to senior citizens and widows; increase in MGNREGA wage rate from Rs.182 to Rs.202 benefiting approximately five crore rural households. Further, under the Prime Minister Kisan Yojana, Rs.2,000 were frontloaded to 8.7 crore beneficiary farmers. For supporting Self-Help Groups (SHGs), the amount of collateral free loans was doubled from Rs. 10 lakh to Rs. 20 lakh. After a while, the Government of India announced an economic package of Rs. 20 lakh crore on 12th May 2020, which included the earlier package of Rs.1.70 lakh crore. This package included Rs. 30,000 crore as an emergency working capital for farmers through National Bank for Agriculture and Rural Development (NABARD) and Rs. 10,000 crore for formalization of micro food enterprises in a cluster based approach. To meet the increased demand for jobs under MGNREGA, the Government of India provided additional Rs. 40,000 crore for the current financial year. Rs. 6,000 crore CAMPA (Compensatory Afforestation Management & Planning Authority) fund was provided for the development of forestry which will benefit tribal population. For businesses and micro, small and medium enterprises (MSMEs) collateral-free automatic loans worth Rs. three lakh crore were earmarked in the form of Guaranteed Emergency Credit Line (GECL) facilities (Reddy and Mamgain, 2020). The Government of India has reduced the burden of EMIs for three months on the people as it will give breathing space to many. Although criticized for paltry cash transfers to poor and affected, above package has started reaching rural population. Government agencies have undertaken record procurement of wheat (38.6 million tonnes of the 2019-20 crop, with minimum support price value of over Rs 74,200 crore) and paddy (74.3 mt, including 15.7 mt after March 31 and worth Rs 28,500 crore). Besides, they have bought about 1.8 mt of chana (valued at Rs 8,750 crore), 0.8 mt of rapeseed-mustard (Rs 3,300 crore) and 0.3 mt of tur/arhar (Rs 1,750 crore). Add the Rs 16,750 crore direct transfers to 8.37 crore farmer accounts as first-installment payment of Rs 2,000 each under the PM-Kisan Samman Nidhi scheme, the total liquidity pumped into the farm economy, post-lockdown, by the government works out to more than Rs 133,000 crore. If the Rs 17,622 crore of wage payments made under MGNREGA from April 1, 2020 is also accounted for, the government's total spend on farmers and rural workers in the past three months will be well in excess of Rs 150,000 crore (Damodaran, 2020). In addition to Central Government's initiatives, State Governments, District administrations, Gram Panchayats and Civil Society Organisations all across the country have proactively taken various measures to check the spread of the COVID-19 pandemic in the country's hinterland. Daily sanitization of public places; establishing shelters and quarantine centres for destitute persons and reverse migrants; providing protective gear, financial assistance and food/ration to the needy; and spreading awareness about the disease are some of those measures. Women SHGs across States have worked tirelessly to overcome shortage of masks, sanitizers and handwash in rural areas, in addition to spreading awareness among villagers (World Bank, 2020). Every crisis also provides an opportunity to think afresh. Current crisis has led to a renewed call for 'Atmanirbhar Bharat' and 'being vocal for local'. If this dream is to become reality, agricultural, farm and non-farm based enterprises and businesses in rural areas have to grow at a faster pace. To enable this, rural infrastructure, skilling of rural youth, rural health, rural education has to be strengthened with revitalized local governance and community participation.

Chapters in the Present Book

Present book is the result of collective efforts of a group of researchers, academicians and development practitioners in studying and analysing challenges, opportunities and responses of different sectors and constituents of rural India amidst Covid-19 and to prescribe policy and operational measures to improve current scenario. Following sections will provide a glimpse of chapters of this book contributed by them.

COVID-19 has impacted various sectors of Indian economy as well. The first lockdown was imposed for 21 days which impacted the lives of many people, communities, urban areas as well as rural areas. Second Chapter titled **'Impact of COVID-19 on Rural Migrants in India' written by Dr. Sakshi Sahni and Dr. Rawal Singh Aulakh** has attempted to study the impacts of COVID 19 on rural migrants in the country from social as well as economic point of view. The plight of the Indian rural migrants was very disheartening to see as they moved back to their native places on foot from large metropolises that were no more supporting them during the lockdown period. They had to face discrimination, stigmatisation trauma as well as poverty during this period. The chapter also discusses various initiatives of the Government and makes policy recommendations for future.

Women are impacted greatly by COVID-19 followed by the lockdown. In India, most of the single women, who are widows and never-married, reside in rural India. The impact of the pandemic and lockdown on less privileged women, from rural backgrounds, has not garnered enough discussion. There are very few studies that specifically focus on single women. Third Chapter titled **'Impact of COVID 19 on Single Women in Rural India' by Mr. Anthony Chettri and Ms. Bedadyuti Jha** explores the plight of four single women across three States and one Union Territory of India through the case-study which narrates their struggles during the lockdown. The major issues emerging from these case studies reveal that single women in rural India are extremely vulnerable to COVID-19, and due to lockdown their capacity to cope with the pandemic have reduced to a large extent. Most of the single women are deprived of benefits from the several social security benefits announced by the governments. The lack of action and initiative by local administration is making it more difficult for them in accessing the government schemes. Unavailability of care support, stigmatization and above all inability to access services like banking or hospitals due to the unavailability of transportation facilities are making the lives and livelihood of single women a big challenge. The chapter recommends that there should be a strategic effort to enhance the awareness level of single women on COVID-19 and that local administration should be sensitive enough to the needs of single women. The Chapter also recommends that the conscious support to restore the livelihood of the single women should find a strategic approach.

Large-scale Indian labour migration to the Gulf countries started in the early 1970s. In every crisis, from Gulf war to now COVID-19, the migrant workers are the most affected as they are left stranded in a foreign land. The majority of the Indian labour migrants in the Gulf are employed in the construction-related sector as semi-skilled and low-skilled workers. The construction sector is the most affected area in every crisis, and it showed an adverse impact on migrant workers. Fourth Chapter titled **'Impact of COVID -19 on Indian Migrant Workers in the Gulf Countries' by Dr. Trilok Chandan Goud** has made an attempt to study the impact of returnee migrants from Gulf region amidst COVID-19. The chapter argues that India faces a big challenge in addressing the issues and problems of the Gulf returnees in this COVID-19 situation. Gulf remittances played an important role in the rural economy of India, particularly in States such as Kerala, Tamil Nadu, Bihar, Uttar Pradesh and Andhra Pradesh. Gulf migrant workers are in a doldrums state and not able to decide whether to return or stay back in the host country. As the employment scenario in the rural areas of their origins in India is bleak due to decreased economic and agricultural activities, those who returned back to their native villages are suffering the double whammy of lost income and burden of repaying debt taken to meet the cost of obtaining visa and job in Gulf region. Chapter recommends measures such as providing financial assistance including loans, skill training for self-employment, and interventions in host countries to ensure access to adequate food, shelter and health facilities to stranded jobless migrants.

The Self Help Groups (SHGs) movement of India has originated from insignificant savings and credit groups that support development of underprivileged rural women into the world's biggest collective of the poor women. Presently, around 67 million women in India are members of six million SHGs. These SHGs have been very helpful in this COVID-19 pandemic. SHGs in Odisha have risen up to the expectations and provided the required support to government and also the rural community. These SHGs have emerged as the real Corona warriors who have contributed immensely in this pandemic. Fifth Chapter titled **'Role Played by Self Help Groups in Combating COVID-19 in Odisha' by Dr. Biswa Mohana Jena and Dr. Binita Nanda** analyses the role played by SHGs in supporting

State government and local administration in meeting gaps in demand and availability of face masks, hand sanitizers and protective equipments; combating misinformation, spreading right awareness; and providing banking and financial solutions to rural communities. The chapter also analyses issues and challenges faced by SHGs and makes recommendations to further improve their effectiveness in combating spread of COVID-19 and making lives of affected rural communities easier.

Panchayati Raj Institutions (PRIs) constitute an essential element of grassroots level of self-governing institutions whose main objective is to work for the welfare of the rural people. It is one of the oldest democratic institutions of India that provides opportunity to the rural people to directly participate in the democratic process of the country. Sixth Chapter titled **'Role of Pachayats Amidst COVID-19: Study of Sonitpur District of Assam' by Mr. Mohan Pathak** has analysed the role played by Panchayats in Assam with special reference to Sonitpur district of Assam based on field study of five GPs. The chapter argues that the Panchayats in India has been playing an important role in preparedness, prevention, and mitigation natural disasters, economic crisis and epidemics. The States like Kerala and Odisha seems to be able to mitigate the pandemic just because of active role of Panchayats. Selected GPs of Sonitpur have formed disaster management committees, organised awareness campaigns, sanitized public places, distributed free ration to poor and migrant labourers, distributed financial assistance announced by Government of India and provided financial assistance to Village Defence Police. Chapter recommends forming permanent disaster management committees at GP level consisting of all elected representatives and key officials in every GP and through these committees GPs to train rural community undertake sanitization, create awareness etc. The chapter also highlights the need to strengthen powers and capacities of PRIs.

Another Chapter on this topic, seventh chapter of this book titled **'Role of Panchayats in Managing COVID-19 in Rural Areas' by Ms. Chitra Chandra** argues that PRIs played a key role in containing the spread of the Corona Virus, limiting the numbers from how gigantic it could have been to what it is now. However, the author says that these key institutions have not found their rightful place in the Disaster Management Act. A passing reference is made to 'local authorities' under section 41 of the DM Act. As per the section, these 'local authorities' including panchayats, municipalities and cantonment boards are mandated to carry out "relief, rehabilitation and reconstruction activities" only under the "directions of the District Authority". The DM Act stipulates, under section 25, the constitution of

'District Disaster Management Authority' under the stewardship of District Collector/ Magistrate who is assisted by the Chairperson of the District Council in the capacity of co-chairperson of the district authority. However, panchayats across India have come up and shouldered significant responsibilities beyond just relief distribution during this unforeseen, unprecedented crisis. They have been forced to step up despite their lack of preparedness for disaster of the order unleashed by the Corona Virus. Even before instructions from central or State governments could reach panchayats, several of them acted on their own to provide food, shelter and support to the vulnerable in the areas.

National Rural Employment Guarantee Act (MGNREGA), 2005 is the largest wage employment programme aimed at reducing distress out-migration, creation of productive community assets and strengthening of panchayats in rural areas in addition to providing employment guarantee for 100 days per household per year. COVID-19 caused by Corona virus has badly impacted the employment scenario in urban as well as rural areas and demand for job under MGNREGA has increased significantly due to migrants returning back to their villages. Responding to the situation, Government of India has provided additional allocation of Rs. 40,000 crore for the implementation of MGNREGA. Eighth Chapter titled **'Impact of COVID-19 on Rural Wage Employment: Analysis of MGNREGA' by Dr. Rajesh Kumar Sinha** makes an attempt to analyse the impact of COVID-19 on rural wage employment and how MGNREGA has come to the rescue of rural population under distress. The chapter also makes recommendations on changes needed in design and processes of MGNREGA implementation amidst the COVID-19 pandemic so that conditions of farmers and manual labourers both can be improved.

In India, the pandemic has impacted the economy very badly which was already under tremendous pressure. Ninth Chapter titled **'Impact of COVID-19 on Rural Economy of India' by Ms. Aninidita Mukherjee** argues that the pandemic has brought about a general starvation, from households to business, and the Governments are also famished. Households in large numbers are starved of jobs and occupation, due to sudden stoppage in production of goods and services, and starved for food also. Firms are capital-starved and government is starved from resources and also from shortage of revenue as every segments of the economy is interconnected to each other. The shutdown of production and other economic activities resulted in hunger for food. Analysing the response, the chapter describes various measures taken by Central and State Governments to redress the distress of the people in terms of distribution of free food grains, free LPG connection, increased allotments and wage rates for MGNREGS, loans for MSMEs, EMI holidays, restructuring of the agricultural sector etc. However the author of the chapter argues that affected people are still facing hunger like situation due to lack of proper implementation of government programmes and recommends that several reform measures are required to make the country self-sufficient which can augment business and strengthen our country.

India has a rich heritage of art and craft making it a potential sector that supplies to both national and international demand. Handicraft forms a precious part of the generational legacy and signifies the richness and diversity of our country through its different elements. The sector is dependent on clusters of artisans, which have their existence marked for centuries. India has 6400 clusters typified as industrial, handicraft and handloom clusters. The sector faces problems like unorganized production, low productivity, inadequate inputs, lack of funding and raw material, weak marketing link, inadequate working capital etc. Tenth Chapter titled **'Impact of COVID-19 on Handicraft Clusters in India' by Ms. Jasmeet Kaur** analyses the impact of COVID-19 on handicraft industry which is the most ancient cottage industry of India based on data collected from relevant academic literature, publications, newspapers, reports. The chapter argues that handicraft clusters are facing shortage of raw material, closed down production place, cancelled orders, no transportation to supply production, deferred payments from suppliers etc. and that handicraft clusters are in highest vulnerability situation due to COVID-19. The Chapter also describes initiatives that have been taken by different stakeholders amidst the pandemic generated crisis.

The motivated, enthusiastic and committed, approximately 690 lakh women members of around 63 lakh Self Help Groups (SHGs) across the country have always contributed in addressing economic and social needs that have emerged at the community level. These women are engaged in livelihoods activities, bringing social change through awareness generation, leading movements and responding during natural calamities. During the on-going COVID-19 crisis also, SHG members have emerged as community warriors by contributing in every possible way to contain the spread of COVID-19. Eleventh Chapter with title **'Impact of COVID-19 on Rural Self Help Groups (SHGs) by Dr. Shafia Wani** describes how SHGs in different parts of country have responded to the COVID-19 crisis by spreading awareness, producing masks & sanitisers, distributing rations/ food to the needy etc. This chapter has specially mentioned contributions of Jammu & Kashmir Rural Livelihoods Mission (JKRLM) amidst COVID-19.

The sudden lockdown implemented by the Government of India created several livelihoods related challenges for rural population for two months. The lockdown created fear among the people and priority was given to save their lives rather than livelihoods. Even the Government of Telangana supplied food grains and financial assistance as per the directions given by the Government of India. The lockdown influenced socio-economic, cultural, psychological, health, hygiene and diet of the people. Besides, all types of educational institutions were closed without any instruction and teaching-learning process got stalled. Twelfth Chapter **'Impact of COVID-19 on Rural Livelihoods: A Sociological Study of Telangana' by Mr. Sreeramulu Gosikonda** analyses the problems of rural people in general and their livelihoods in particular that have arises due to lockdown. The chapter is based on empirical research conducted in a village in Telangana through personal interviews with the respondents. The chapter observes that the lockdown has hit rural livelihoods adversely. It recommends that for revival of the rural economy and livelihoods effective implementation of policies and programmes announced by the central and State government is imperative.

Majority of India lives in villages and rural education in India is of utmost importance. Education at the elementary level serves as the catalyst in the growth of a child from being a novice to become a person with the knowledge and skills required for him to contribute positively to the society. With the spread of the COVID-19, the worst affected education sector stakeholders are school-going children. The lockdown has interrupted learning activities of school going children. Poor quality of educators, poor infrastructure, lack of financial support and access to quality learning are the major bottlenecks of rural education in India. Thirteenth Chapter titled **'Impact of COVID-19 on Rural Education in India' by Dr. Rajeev Bansal** gives a background of rural education, elementary education envisaged in Sustainable Development Goals (SDGs) and status of rural education in India. It takes into account the impact of COVID-19 on rural education, status of information, communication and technology at this threshold. The status of digital literacy with internet usage besides academic loss and digital divide in rural education sector have been analysed as key impact of COVID-19 in this chapter. With the help of case studies the chapter has analysed challenges faced, responses as well as the suggestion to address the situation.

We all live in a society where 'interaction' and 'interdependence' with each other is important to survive as no one is self-sufficient. Society is a network of inter-relationship in which every institution including socio-economic, political, educational and the health sector of a particular society is 'interdependent' with one another to function as a whole. If one part of the society is disrupted, it affects the other parts also that lead to the pathological stage. Unquestionably, the COVID-19 has affected the lives of people in many aspects which are yet to be adequately studied. Fourteenth Chapter with title **'Impact of COVID-19 on Rural Society of Sikkim' by Ms. Jashi M. Gurung** has highlighted the impact and challenges faced by the rural society of Sikkim caused by the COVID-19. The chapter is based on review of literature secondary sources such as News channels of Sikkim, journals, official documents, and articles on COVID-19 coupled with a primary study. The Chapter recommends that along with government officials, health workers, police, media, etc., each need to act responsibly for a better response to COVID-19 by rural society.

The MGNREGA in 2020 got a new fillip as lakhs of migrants started returning to their villages from thickly populated urban centers where COVID-19 was spreading fast. Fifteenth Chapter of the book titled **'MGNREGA and Social Audit amidst COVID-19' written by Dr. Vikash Jha** argues that nearly sixty lakhs villagers returned to their villages in Uttar Pradesh and Bihar in the period April – June 2020. These villagers required livelihood options as they were in distress and had run out of savings. MGNREGA in past had stood test of times in providing employment was the program which could be relied upon by the government as 'system' of implementing the program was in place. The selection of works by Gram Panchayats, approval by block offices, funds allocation, job card registration and payment methods, all these critical components were in place which made it easier for the government to implement the program. Nearly 1.21 crores people were provided employment in the period April – June 2020 in UP and Bihar. It mitigated the pains of COVID-19 to some extent. The fast allocation and expenditure on the program threw up challenges for social audit. The social audit process could not be carried out in a normal way due to restrictions of COVID-19. Hence the social audit in both the states in 2020 fell behind. The need of the hour to strengthen the social audit process by using emerging new technologies such as social media and online platform so that huge expenditure does not go unverified and good assets are created in the villages.

References

Amrita News Service. (2020). Study of Impact of COVID-19 on Rural Communities. Amritaworld.org, May 6. Retrieved from https://amritaworld.org/disaster-relief/study-of-impact-of-COVID-19-on-rural-communities/ on 21.08.2020

Bhavani, R.V. (2020). Impact of COVID-19 on Rural Lives and Livelihoods. ORF, New Delhi. Retrieved from https://www.orfonline.org/expert-speak/impact-covid19-rural-lives-livelihoods-india-64889/ on 20.08.2020.

Damodaran, Harish. (2020). Rs 150,000 crore plus: the govt stimulus for rural areas post lockdown. Indian Express. June 25, New Delhi. Retrieved from https://indianexpress.com/article/explained/rs-150000-crore-plus-the-govt-stimulus-for-rural-areas-post-lockdown-6474873/ on 22.08.2020.

Gera, Ishaan (2020). COVID-19 Spreading in Rural India: Villages, Semi-urban Areas Account for Half of New cases. Financial Express, August 11. Retrieved from https://www.financialexpress.com/lifestyle/health/covid-spread-rural-semi-urban-areas-account-for-half-of-all-fresh-cases-now/2051034/ on 11.08.2020.

Khan, T. (2020). How COVID-19 Is Impacting Rural Market. Financial Express, April 26. Retrieved from https://www.financialexpress.com/brandwagon/how-COVID-19-is-impacting-the-rural-market/1940102/ on 20.08.2020.

Ministry of Information and Broadcasting. (2020). India's Response to Covid Outbreak. Government of India, New Delhi. Retrieved from https://pib.gov.in/PressReleasePage.aspx?PRID=1608727 on 20.08.2020.

Mitra, Shouvik. (2020). Implication of COVID-19 for Rural India. IDR. Retrieved from https://idronline.org/the-implications-of-COVID-19-for-rural-india/ on 20.08.2020.

Nair, K.R. (2020). Impact of COVID-19 on Rural India. Diplomatist, April 30. Retrieved from https://diplomatist.com/2020/04/30/impact-of-COVID-19-on-rural-india/ on 21.08.2020

Pradhan, Vibhudatta (2020). Crowded Villages Show Why Coronavirus Cases are Surging in Rural India. Business Standard, August 11. Retrieved from https://www.business-standard.com/article/current-affairs/crowded-villages-show-why-coronavirus-cases-are-surging-in-rural-india-120080800173_1.html on 11.08.20220.

Reddy W.R. and Mamgai R.P. (2020). Revival and Reconstruction of Rural Livelihoods Amidst COVID-19: Policy Responses, Opportunities and Way Ahead. National Institute of Rural Development and Panchayati Raj, Hyderabad.

Sengupta, S. (2020). How Can We Save Rural India From COVID-19. Down To Earth, May 20. Retrieved from https://www.downtoearth.org.in/blog/water/how-can-we-save-rural-india-from-COVID-19-71265 on 21.08.2020.

Shylendra HS. (2020). How Is COVID-19 Playing Out in Rural Areas? The Hindu BusinessLine, May 25. Retrieved from https://www.thehindubusinessline.com/opinion/how-is-COVID-19-playing-out-in-rural-india/article31671013.ece on 20.08.2020.

WHO. (2020a). Naming the Coronavirus Disease (COVID-19) and the Virus that Causes it. Retrieved from https://www.who.int/emergencies/diseases/novel-coronavirus-2019/technical-guidance/naming-the-coronavirus-disease-(covid-2019)-and-the-virus-that-causes-it on 20.08.2020.

WHO. (2020b). Corono Virus. Retrieved from https://www.who.int/health-topics/coronavirus#tab=tab_1 on 20.08.2020.

World Bank. (2020). In India, Women's Self-Help Groups Combat the COVID-19 (Corona Virus) Pandemic. Retrieved from https://www.worldbank.org/en/news/feature/2020/04/11/women-self-help-groups-combat-covid19-coronavirus-pandemic-india on 22.08.2020.

Chapter - 2

Impact of COVID-19 on Rural Migrants in India

— Dr. Sakshi Sahni ,
Dr. Rawal Singh Aulakh

What is novel Corona Virus or COVID-19?

According to World Health Organization (WHO) website, "*on 31 December 2019, WHO was informed and learnt of cases of pneumonia of unknown cause in Wuhan City, China*". A novel coronavirus was recognized and acknowledged as the basis by Chinese authorities on 7 January 2020 and was temporarily named "2019-nCoV." Coronaviruses (CoV) are a major group of viruses that cause infection fluctuating from the common cold to more severe diseases and extreme maladies. A novel coronavirus (nCoV) is a new tension and pressure that has not been formerly known in the past to the individuals (WHO).

The appearance and development of the current worldwide pandemic, COVID-19, has so far been a danger as well as risk to the worldwide network of citizens (Buhejietal. 2020). COVID-19 or novel coronavirus is a variant of the corona group of viruses which causes infection called SARS on the individuals they contaminate (Buhejietal, 2020). The virus is primarily transmitted through coughing or sneezing on individuals (Buhejietal, 2020). Sengupta and Jha (2020) states that the pandemic caused by the coronavirus disease (COVID 19), the severest wellbeing crisis of our times, is ready to disturb social, economic and political systems and lives around the world. In this chapter, the impact of corona virus on social and economic system on rural migrants in India will be covered. With the absence of any reasonable immunization, most governments have compulsory executed forced lockdowns to control the development of the virus causing infection (Buhejietal, 2020).

How India responded to COVID-19?

Prime Minister Narendra Modi imposed a 21-day compulsory lockdown from March 24, 2020 and motivated Indians to rehearse as well as practice of social separating and hand hygiene through washing hands frequently (Nilsen, 2020). He requested the individuals to remain at any place wherever they are (Nilsen, 2020). Sengupta and Jha (2020) states that as preventive moderation measures, India started strict controls since March 2020, requesting 1.3 billion individuals to remain at home for the time period of lockdown except if engaged in allowed essential and basic services. Through a mix of control actions that included constraint on movement and shutting of manufacturing factories and work environments, nations are attempting and working to "flatten the curve" that is decreasing the figure of COVID 19 cases and to prevent the clogging and collapse of healthcare system of India (Sengupta and Jha, 2020). A question still remains in the mind of the authors that "*Who are more vulnerable to this virus?*". The migrant labourers or workers are considered to be the most vulnerable to this virus. Hence, the chapter will focus on rural migrants and its impacts.

What was the plight of rural migrants in India?

The effect of lockdown knocked out the rural migrants considerably (Poornima, Kumar, 2020). The lockdown across the country has caught the people and the government at crossroads (Poornima, Kumar, 2020). The agony, abandonment, worry, rage, suffering, frustration and adversities experienced and felt by the migrant workers are beyond conception (Poornima, Kumar, 2020). When the lockdown was imposed, the nation's 120 million migrant workers, still, did not comply by the Prime Minister's demand as well as request and begun advancing back from India's super urban metro and mega cities to their native villages by walking interstate highways (Nilsen, 2020). Their employment dissipated and disappeared in just few days and work just vanished (Nilsen, 2020).

The central government declared the lockdown on 24 March 2020 to stop the spread of COVID-19, subsequently millions of migrant labours were enforced out of works and occupation with no means of earning a living, began fleeing the cities. In no time, they found themselves undesirable as well as unwanted in the metropolises they shaped and constructed with their labour (Poornima, Kumar, 2020). The pictures of men, women and children walking back hundreds of miles to their villages are still new and fresh in remembrance (Poornima, Kumar, 2020). Many newspapers, print media, social media and TV channels showed the irony of walking barefoot to their native places. Many migrant workers marched or walked for days on end, covering hundreds of kilometres with their kith and kin (Nilsen, 2020). Many left for their journey without adequate food and found themselves at the less than desirable finish of brutal and mortifying treatment (Nilsen, 2020). Numerous additionally passed away on their way home (Nilsen, 2020). Banakar (2020) of the Indian Express states that the phase 3 of the lockdown in India, which was stretched from May 4 to May 17, brought in the demise of 118 migrant labours, the maximum and greatest amongst all other lockdown periods, data from Save Life Foundation has uncovered. The phase 3 added to almost nearly 60 percent of all migrant employee demises during the lockdown, while phases one, two and four witnessed 25, 17 and 38 deaths correspondingly (Banakar, 2020). World Bank has expressed and stated that the across the country lockdown in India had impacted about 40 million internal migrants inside one month of its commencement (Business Today, April 23, 2020). Around 50,000 to 60,000 people moved from urban centres like mega and metro cities to rural areas of origin in the range of a couple of days (ibid). According to the report- "COVID 19 Crisis through a Migration Lens"- the scale of internal migration is about two and a half times that of international migration (ibid).

According to Gulf news, a newspaper read that "India is walking home" concerning to huge number ranging from hundreds of thousands of migrant workers and labourers back home after Prime Minister Narendra Modi's declaration of a nationwide lockdown on March 23 (Das Sanjib, May 2020). Das further states that according to one estimate, by the night of March 25, when the lockdown was hardly 24 hours old, 60000 migrant workers were now on their way back home from several mega cities and metro towns across the nation. With all trains and other mass transit services having by now come to an unending halt, the torment and experience of individuals who had set by walking on foot out of complete fear and urgency had recently started (Das, 2020). According to Sengupta and Jha, (2020) as millions of migrants workforces in India started their walk home journey, carrying families, grasping their scanty belongings, flocking and swarming in disturbed transportation networks, resourceless, after the unexpected and abrupt lockdown in the wake of the novel coronavirus pandemic they confronted hunger, poverty, the anger, fierceness and rage of the police and doubt of societies and sad heart breaking death (Ghosh, 2020; Jadhav, 2020; Jha & Pankaj, 2020 cited in Sengupta and Jha, 2020).

Who are the migrant labourers in India?

Das (2020) states that the migrant labourers are individuals who travel from their States of residence or so-called domicile to other States in the nation looking for employments and a job. In India, relocation of workers has been occurring for over a century, nonetheless the numbers have seen an exponential increase over the most recent 30 years (Das, 2020). The greater part of these migrants are daily wage employees and comprise the massive unorganised or informal sector that is set apart by low salaries, hostile and unfavourable working hours, absence of any work contract at all and non-appearance of any social wellbeing or worker welfare scheme or worker government assistance collaborative (Das, 2020). With little or nothing to show for any formal education and coming mostly from destitute or poor families and upbringings, these migrants are frequently hired in lowly jobs (Das, 2020). These migrant workers contribute about 10% of the country's gross domestic product (Das, Sengupta and Jha, 2020).

India's poverty profile

According to World bank on their website infographic India's Poverty Profile published on May 27, 2016 although four years old which states the data of 2012 stating that 270,000,000 (27 crores) Indians are poor which means that 1 in 5 Indians is poor. The seven low income States house 62% of India's poor and these are home to 45% of India's population. 80% of India's poor live in rural areas. The seven States are described in the table below:

State	*Number of poor (In millions)*
Uttar Pradesh	60
Bihar	36
Madhya Pradesh	24
Odisha	14
Jharkhand	13
Rajasthan	10
Chattisgarh	10

(Source: World Bank: https://www.worldbank.org/en/news/infographic/2016/05/27/india-s-poverty-profile)

The above table gives a clear picture of the scenario of poverty 8 years ago. With the coming of COVID 19, the scenario would have gone worse than the one depicted above as due to lack of data the current picture of this for year 2020 is not available.

Issues and impacts of COVID-19 on rural migrants

There are various issues and impacts faced by rural migrants. The authors have classified them into social and economic effects.

(1) Social Impacts

(a) ***Anxiety and mental health of rural migrants-*** According to Choudhary, (2020) during the lockdown time of India, across the country abrupt bans on movement, absence of work led to no money or finance related means to deal with day to day food costs and isolation rules as well as maintain social distancing, all have brought about significant levels of nervousness, anxiety which hence initiated socially unreliable conduct and fits of anxiety as well as panic attacks among inner transient or migrant workers (Choudhary, 2020). Rccent escape of abandoned internal migrant workers to railroad stations and transport stations like bus stands, making urgent endeavours to return to their home states disregarding lockdown rules is a case of this (Choudhary, 2020). This constantly brings about the endless loop of helplessness to contamination, isolation, stress, and infringement of preventive measures (Choudhary, 2020). Nervousness levels and anxiety are to be sure structure in these migrant laborers, constraining a considerable lot of them to travel a few a thousand kilometres by walking on foot to arrive at their local native places with no arrangement of food or shelter in the travel (Choudhary, 2020).

(b) ***Lack of alertness, awareness, frightened or careless and negligent behaviour-*** According to Ganguly et.al. (2020) the deadly contest against extremely infectious and spreadable COVID-19 strains and acclaims the essence of collaboration as well as assistance from every person of the humanity and solidarity among the inhabitants across the various socio-economic classes. However, a range of reported incidents as mentioned in the section of plight of Indian rural migrants exhibits the lack of responsiveness, vulnerability on the one hand, but sheer negligence and irresponsible behaviour is also, evident (Ganguly, 2020). The reason can also be a previous policy, plan as well as approach dealing with migrants, workers in informal sector, and income options for daily wage employees, migrant workers was completely missing from the Government side (Ganguly et.al., 2020).

(c) ***Stigmatisation-*** World Health Organization states that social stigma or disgrace in milieu of health is the negative affiliation between an individual or cluster of people who share certain features and a particular illness (WHO). In an epidemic, this may mean calling people by labels, typecast, distinguished against, treated separately, and/or experience loss of status because of an

apparent link with an illness. Such treatment can negatively disturb those with the sickness, as well as their caregivers, households, supports and communities (WHO). Individuals who don't have the illness but share other characteristics with this bunch may too endure from shame. The current COVID-19 outbreak has triggered and flared up the social stigma and prejudiced oppressive practises against folks of certain ethnic foundations as well as anybody seen to have been in contact with the infection (WHO). Mohanty and Kumar, (2020) in an article in Hindustan Times states that migrant workers and their families have been singled out, scoffed or ridiculed at, and irritated by villagers. In a few villages, they confront exclusion indeed after completing the required 14-day isolation period. Migrant workers returning from India's industrial states are fighting stigma and bias in their home villages in some parts of Uttar Pradesh, Jharkhand and Odisha because local residents were suspicious that the migrant workers are possible carriers of the coronavirus causing COVID-19. According to Print, (Mishra, 2020) states that in Patna that rural migrants returning from Delhi were subject to "social boycott". Mishra further states that the social stigma is so strong that these migrant workers coming from outside are facing HIV like stigma and no one likes to go near them.

(2) Economic Impacts

(a) ***Unemployment and Poverty-*** About 450 million informal workers comprising 90% of India's workforce were not permitted to have paid leaves (Sengupta, Jha, 2020). A larger part of them are migrant workers who are at the edge of the emergency or catastrophe during the lockdown when work from home becomes the new normal throughout the globe due to the epidemic. Numerous among these inter-state migrants picked to walk hundreds of kilometres in the hope to reach to their native places (Slater et.al. 2020). Among them, the terror of staying hungry over day-to-day wage loss overshadowed their anxiety and distress of the virus (Ganguly, 2020).

(b) ***Homelessness-*** Habib et.al. (2020, New York Times) states that India as of now had one of the world's biggest destitute populaces, and the lockdown has expanded its numbers exponentially, workers for nongovernmental organization state. A 2011 government census put the sum of homeless at 1.7 million, almost certainly a

vast underestimate in this country of 1.3 billion, experts say (Habib et.al., 2020, New York Times). For the most part, the impoverished and homeless are taken care of by India's variety of religious foundations as well as institutions like the Temples, Gurudwaras and Mosques. In any case, due to COVID 19 presently, everything is shut, and homeless are feeling the strain (Habib et.al., 2020, New York Times).

(c) ***Debt Traps*** – Poor helpless families are enforced to borrow at inflated interest rates and loan costs from private money lenders in form of cash and hence suffer unspeakable bullying, intimidation, terrorizing, animosity and aggression in the event of non-payment (the newsminute.com). During the time of COVID 19 emergency, when there is barely any job of source of income, borrowing dependence has been huge especially among rural migrants' segment of population (the newsminute.com).

(d) ***Reverse migration*** – In large parts of the country, the coronavirus pandemic has activated a huge reverse migration from the city to rural areas (Singh, 2020). Hundreds of thousands of rural migrants parading back to their native places were outpoured on the Indian highways to find some compassion and sympathy (Dandekar and Ghai, 2020 cited in Singh, 2020).Demography, social and economy of rural India will be highly impacted by the involuntary reverse migration from city to rural areas (Singh, 2020). In order to search for better employment opportunities these rural migrant workers who were peripheral marginal workers in the past left agriculture, farming and moved to metropolitan areas for. The forced and involuntary reverse migration in the midst of agrarian emergency represents a major danger on individuals to fall into wretched destitution (Singh 2020). This in turn will pose a big challenge on the economy of rural India (Singh, 2020).

In the current circumstance, the interior transient workers in India is around 450 million. Ground reality show transient works are higher in the states of UP and Bihar followed by MP, Punjab, Rajasthan, Uttarakhand, Jammu and Kashmir and West Bengal (Sing, 2020). Presently, returnees are returning with no resulting in poverty and hunger. As per ILO gauges around 400 million specialists in India in the casual economy are at the danger of falling further into destitution during the emergency of the pandemic (Singh, 2020).The reverse migration will additionally result in to fall in the producer cost of yields which will decrease farm wages and salary. Then again, because of low efficiency and storing of food articles, there will be an ascent in the costs of food things which will significantly influence needy individuals (Singh, 2020).

Government Initiatives

Pradhan Mantri Garib Kalyan Yojana (PMGKY)

The central and states government in India under the distinct economic package, Pradhan Mantri Garib Kalyan Yojna (PMGKY) scheme etc. attempted to deal with the economy and the least fortunate among the poor yet successful execution of this package represents a major test as well as challenge (Singh, 2020 cites Jha 2020).

The Ministry of Finance on their official website on the press release states that 42 crore poor people have received financial assistance of 65,454 crore under the above-mentioned scheme as on 20June, 2020 (pib.gov.in). As a part of the scheme, the Government announced free food grains and cash payment to women and poor senior citizens and farmers. The central and state governments are continuously monitoring the implementation of the package (pib.gov.in). The Government also announced free food grains supply and chana to migrants for two months as on 19th June, 2020 (pib.gov.in). The other examples include, Rs. 500 deposit to jan dhan accounts of women, additional allocation to MGNREGA for jobs to returned migrants, credit facilities, package for revival of economy so that migrants can get back their job etc. The table below describes the benefits

Pradhan Mantri Garib Kalyan Package:
Direct Benefit Transfer till 19/06/2020

Scheme	*Number of Beneficiaries*	*Amount*
Support to PMJDY women account holders	1st Ins - 20.65 Cr (100%) 2ndIns –20.63 Cr 3rd Ins -20.62 (100%)	1stIns –10,325 Cr 2ndIns – 10,315 Cr 3rd Ins –10,312 Cr
Support to NSAP (Aged widows, Divyang, Senior citizen)	2.81 Cr (100%)	2814 Cr
Front-loaded payments to farmers under PM-KISAN	8.94 Cr	17891 Cr
Support to Building & Other Construction workers	2.3 Cr	17891 Cr
24% contribution to EPFO	66 Cr	996 Cr
Ujjwala	1st Ins – 7.48 2nd Ins – 4.48	8488 Cr
TOTAL	42.84 Cr	65,454 Cr

Source: Ministry of Finanace, GOI, Press Release https://pib.gov.in/PressReleasePage.aspx?PRID=1632863)

Policy Recommendations

There are brief policy recommendations and suggestions to improve condition of migrants amidst COVID-19:

1. Promotion of infrastructure development in rural areas for multiplier effect-by strengthening rural infrastructure to promote growth of agro-based industries, better access to markets for farmers and creation of job opportunities for the rural population (Narang, KPMG, 2020).
2. Creation of non-farm employment opportunities such as encouraging setting up food/agri processing units, diversification of agriculture with crop diversification. Promote modern integrated cold chain (from farm to processing facility to retail outlet), set up pre-processing centres and pre-cooling facilities near farms and mandis, encourage investor-friendly food parks, upgrade food processing clusters, modernise agriculture markets/ warehouses and abattoirs (GOI, Rabco. 2005).
3. Prioritisation of health infrastructure with focus on rural areas.
4. Re-skilling of returned migrants with skills required in rural areas.
5. Portability of ration cards/health cards/pensions/fellowship etc so that even migrating to other States does not hamper social security benefits.
6. Proper utilisation of welfare fund collected under Building and Construction Workers (regulation of employment and conditions of service) Act 1996 which remains underutilised.

Conclusion

There was failure of Indian side where a prior strategy dealing with migrants, employees in informal sector, and livelihood options for daily wage earners, migrant workers was completely missing (Ganguly et.al., 2020). There was an absence of appropriate preparation before the first declaration of the nationwide lockdown on 24 March, 2020 thereby resulting in discrimination among rural migrants, overall health and well-being of rural migrants deteriorated in absence of any measures taken by the Government. These rural migrants were facing social pressure of poverty, loss of livelihood, stigmatisation and were alienated by the countrymen left alone on roads to meet their fate where many of rural migrants lost their lives. Although the Government initiatives were taken, but they came very late and many migrants had to lose their lives while going back home.

The truth is that rural migrants are very important and vital part of our economy without which both rural and urban areas will not be able to sustain.

References

Banakar Pushkar, (2020 June 3) Most migrants died during COVID-19 lockdown 3.0: SaveLife Foundationhttps://www.newindianexpress.com/nation/2020/jun/03/most-migrants-died-during-COVID-19-lockdown-30-savelife-foundation-2151565.html

Buheji, M., da Costa Cunha, K., Beka, G., Mavriæ, B., Leandro do Carmo de Souza, Y., Souza da Costa Silva, S.,… ChetiaYein, T. (2020). The Extent of COVID-19 Pandemic Socio-Economic Impact on Global Poverty. A Global Integrative Multidisciplinary Review. American Journal of Economics, 2020(4), 213–224. https://doi.org/10.5923/j.economics.20201004.02

Choudhary, R. (2020). COVID 19 pandemic: Mental health challenges of internal migrant workers of India. *Asian Journal of Psychiatry*, *54*. https://doi.org/10.1016/j.ajp.2020.102254

Choudhary P.R, Ghosh R.K, Sindhi S(2020) Covid 19 Crisis, Pademic Resilience and Linkages to Land: An exposition. Indian Institute of Management, Ahmedabad. Working Paper 2020-05-01

Das Sanjeeb Kumar (2020) COVID-19: The 'invisible' Indians: Story of the 'great migration'https://gulfnews.com/world/asia/india/COVID-19-the-invisible-indians-story-of-the-great-migration-1.71554678

Ganguly, M., Goli, S., Ganguly, D., &Misra, S. (2020). Munich Personal RePEc Archive India's COVID-19 Episode: Resilience, Response, Impact and Lessons. https://mpra.ub.uni-muenchen.de/99691/

G.R. Poornima, M.N. Kumar Suresh. (2020). Corona India and Mass Migration: Unfolding Implications for the Present and the future. MuktShabadJournal.IX,VI, p. 1514.

Iyengar, K., Mabrouk, A., Jain, V. K., Venkatesan, A., & Vaishya, R. (2020). Learning opportunities from COVID-19 and future effects on health care system. *Diabetes & metabolic syndrome*, *14*(5), 943–946. Advance online publication. https://doi.org/10.1016/j.dsx.2020.06.036

Kumar Chandan, Mohanty Debashish (2020) May 11. Hindustan Times Migrant workers battle stigma, bias back home. https://www.hindustantimes.com/india-news/migrant-workers-battle-stigma-bias-back-home/story-0uuRSEZfoickVOrPU2agGL.html accessed on August7, 2020.

Maria Abi-Habib and Sameer Yasir March 29, 2020 Newyork Times https://www.nytimes.com/2020/03/29/world/asia/coronavirus-india-migrants.html

Nilsen Alf Gunvald,2020, Covid 19 and India's Development Crisis. African HSS Responses www.nihss.ac.za/hssresponse

Ministry of Finanace, GOI, Press Releasehttps://pib.gov.in/PressReleasePage.aspx?PRID=1632863

Ministry of Food Processing Industries GOI, Rabo India Finanace Private Limited Visison, (2005) strategy and Action Plan for food processing Industries in India https://mofpi.nic.in/sites/default/files/volume1.pdf_0.pdf

Mishra Dipak. The Print (2020) 31 st March No one wants to go near them – returning migrant workers in Bihar faces social boycott. https://theprint.in/india/no-one-wants-to-go-near-them-returning-migrant-workers-in-bihar-face-social-boycott/392081/

Narang Puneet, (2020) July 1, Reviving the Indian economy- Does infrastructure hold the key? KPMGhttps://home.kpmg/in/en/home/insights/2020/07/reviving-the-indian-economy.htm

Richa Mukhra, Kewal Krishan, Tanuj Kanchan COVID-19 Sets off Mass Migration in India.

Arch Med Res. 2020 Jun 6 doi: 10.1016/j.arcmed.2020.06.003 [Epub ahead of print]PMCID: .PMC7275149

Sengupta Sohini, Jha M.K. (2020). Social PolicyCOVID 19 and impoverished migrants:Challenges and prospects in Locked Down India. The International Journal of Community and Social Development 2(2). Sage publications

Singh Bhanu Paratap (2020).Impact of COVID-19 on Rural Economy in India. Banaras Hindu University, India .Munich Personal RePEcArchive https://mpra.ub.uni-muenchen.de/100530/1/MPRA_paper_100526.pdf

Slater J, Masih N (2020) March 28 In India, the world's biggest lockdown has forced migrants to walk hundreds of miles homehttps://www.washingtonpost.com/world/asia_pacific/india-coronavirus-lockdown-migrant-workers/2020/03/27/a62df166-6f7d-11ea-a156-0048b62cdb51_story.html

The Lancet (2020). India under COVID-19 lockdown. *Lancet (London, England)*, *395*(10233), 1315. https://doi.org/10.1016/S0140-6736(20)30938-7

http://www.euro.who.int/en/health-topics/health-emergencies/coronavirus-COVID-19/novel-coronavirus-2019-ncov

https://www.who.int/healthy_settings/types/cities/en/

https://www.businesstoday.in/current/economy-politics/coronavirus-lockdown-in-india-has-affected-40-million-migrants-says-world-bank/story/401762.html

https://www.worldbank.org/en/news/infographic/2016/05/27/india-s-poverty-profile

https://timesofindia.indiatimes.com/blogs/red-button-day-light/estimation-and-skill-mapping-of-migrant-workers/

https://www.who.int/publications/m/item/a-guide-to-preventing-and-addressing-social-stigma-associated-with-COVID-19?gclid=EAIaIQobChMIwOuI9KKI6wIV2bWWCh3XNAbPEAAYASAAEgK8tfD_BwE

https://www.voanews.com/COVID-19-pandemic/pandemic-triggers-reverse-migration-india-cities-villages

https://www.thenewsminute.com/article/COVID-19-creating-new-debt-traps-poor-indian-families-128189

Chapter - 3

Impact of COVID 19 on Single Women in Rural India

— *Mr. Anthony Chettri,*
Ms. Bedadyuti Jha

Introduction

The year 2020 marks the twenty-fifth anniversary of the *Fourth World Conference on Women* and adoption of the *Beijing Declaration and Platform for Action* (1995), which were intended to be the ground-breaking instruments for gender equality and especially safeguarding the rights of the women. But with the pandemic of COVID 19 followed by lockdown, the limited gains that the world achieved in safeguarding the rights of the women are at the risk of being withdrawn. This pandemic is increasing and deepening the rift of pre-existing gender inequalities and amplifying the socio-economic and political vulnerabilities not only among women but also among the transgenders and people with disabilities. This paper will try to summarise with the impact of COVID 19 on the lives and livelihood of Single Women through the process of documenting a few case studies. (*CSW64 / Beijing + 25 (2020) | Commission on the Status of Women | UN Women – Headquarters*, n.d.)

The gendered impact of COVID-19 has been discussed at length. However, most of such discussions have been focused on urban middle-class women's struggle during the pandemic of managing the increased burden of household responsibilities while juggling the pressure to retain their optimum productivity at work. The impact of the pandemic and lockdown on less privileged women, from rural backgrounds, have not garnered enough discussion. The larger discussions on the gendered impact of COVID-19 also tends to exclude the narratives of the transgender communities. The struggles of the transgender communities are gendered nonetheless and also are intersectional of their other social markers such as caste, class etc in play.

Along with the whole world, the Indian government has taken all the necessary steps/measures to ensure that the spread of the virus (COVID 19) is curtailed to a large extent. But the measures were taken from a very patriarchal and elitist perspective. No one can forget the scenario of bags perched on the heads of the migrant workers and children in their arms walking desperately down the highways to return to their villages, hundreds of miles away, just the day after the lockdown was declared. The government never could fathom in their wildest imagination that such a scene will be there on the streets. The state failed the migrant workers. (*The Pandemic Exposes India's Apathy Toward Migrant Workers - The Atlantic*, n.d.)

Similarly, just after the lockdown, we noticed a sharp rise in the violence against women and child abuse. The chart on this page shows that there is a sharp increase in the complaints related to gender-based violence. India, unfortunately, is not an exception to the global trend of increased pandemic induced domestic violence.

The concerns of the marginalized sections of a population often get overlooked in the larger policy discourse all over the globe and India is not an exception. Lower representation of marginalized groups in the decision making bodies, inherent discriminations and prejudices present in cultures against marginalized populations often play a role in the indifference towards the concerns of the most marginalised and resultantly the most vulnerable communities. With the onset of COVID-19, there is a new challenge in front of policymakers and civil society organizations to include these communities whose vulnerabilities have increased manifolds under this pandemic. In this background, Indo Global Social Service Society (IGSSS) has made this study with an aim to understand the impact of the COVID-19 pandemic and the subsequent nationwide lockdowns that were imposed nationwide to keep the outbreak of COVID on the lives and livelihood of Single women.

Background and Rationale

The sudden imposition of the nationwide on March 24, 2020 left the majority of the population with less than four hours to prepare for 21 days long period which subsequently was extended. This time was severely inadequate for everyone to prepare themselves, and those with additional vulnerabilities were the most impacted.

Objectives and Methodology

The main objectives of this research are: 1. Assessing the impact of COVID-19 pandemic and subsequent lockdown on the lives and livelihoods of single women; 2. Understanding gaps in existing policies targeted at them and their implementation and efficiency on the grassroots level and 3. Suggesting changes in existing policies at the formulation and implementation levels, and newer policies to national-level stakeholders in the policy domain.

The study was conducted using a qualitative approach with case study technique. The choice of a qualitative approach was done considering the subjective realities of single women as a vulnerable group. The study was conducted mainly to understand the experiences of participants who were living through multiple layers of coexisting realities. In the current crisis of COVID-19, the target population continues to go through multiple kinds of violence which are layered in terms of geographical regions, caste, gender beyond binaries, cultural and social differences etc. Hence it was important to understand that the exploratory nature of the study through case studies of the respondent would unearth the social, cultural and economic realities of the respondents which would help the research team to negotiate for the policies which are inclusive and sustainable and also help to bridge the societal gaps.

All the answers were collected by IGSSS employees from locations where IGSSS is working either through partner-led projects or through Direct Implementation projects. The sampling method used was snowball sampling. In the case studies, complete anonymity has been maintained about the respondents and they have been assigned a representative Code to protect their identity.

Four Case Studies of Single Women

Single women in India are an often-ignored section of women. According to a report in The Times of India, the number of single women in India is about 7.1 Crore among which 1.3 crores are widows and 1.2 crores have never married. Among the 7.1 crores, only 2.5 crores live in urban areas. The majority of single women, 4.6 crores live in rural areas. In the mainstream discussions, even on the gendered impact of the pandemic, single women are an extremely invisible section. In the case of the minuscule discussions that happen on single women, it is usually focused on the urban middle-class single women and the majority of them away from the urban landscape remain absent from the discussion. (*Why the Lockdown Is Harder on Single Women - Times of India*, n.d.)

While conducting the study, we reached out to single women in several states and tried to capture their struggles in this pandemic and lockdown. We will be presenting these narratives in the form of case studies.

Case Study 1: Location, Maharashtra

The respondent is a widow and lives in a rural area close to Mumbai, Maharashtra. She said that through news she came to know that a disease has spread and everybody has to wear a mask and gloves. And in the beginning, only her Basti was locked down as one case appeared in there. By that time her employer asked her not to come for work where she works as a domestic worker and cook but they have provided her with half salary for the two months that she has not been going to work, so she has had the money for her sustenance.

She lives with her daughter in rented accommodation, but they have managed to pay the rent so there is no problem of eviction looming over their head. She said that as a single woman she at present is not facing much difficulty in accessing basic essential items as her employer has paid her half salary and many NGOs have provided relief kits etc.

She said that she had not enrolled for widow pension as she wasn't aware of it. She said that she has hardly gone out in the last two months so she does not have any ideas about what facilities are available nearby such as PHC etc.

She said that even though she has not lost her job, many women in her Basti who work as domestic workers and other informal work have lost their jobs. She said that she did not have any idea about when things will become normal after the pandemic. As per suggestions for the government, she said the price of the essential items are increasing such as rice and vegetables and people are losing their livelihood in the pandemic. According to her, the government should do something to address that.

Case Study 2: Location: Raipur, Chhattisgarh

The respondent is a widow living in Odiya Basti, rural Raipur, Chattisgarh. She said that she heard about COVID-19 from people discussing it. She knows this is a contagious disease for which the government has asked people to stay at home, put a mask in the face, wash hands, keep the house clean etc. The respondent said that she lives alone and works at 3 households as a domestic worker She said she only had rice, with no money to buy the rest of the food. Her work had stopped. Otherwise, where she used to work, her employers used to help by giving some money and vegetables. But now with lockdown, there is no means to go out. She also said that LPG gas is not free for everyone and she has not enough money to fill gas. It is also difficult to get wood from outside to burn the stove.

She said that as a single woman, she is facing some difficulties. When there is no help in the house and there is no arrangement to run the stove, then she went to the government facility to get cooked food in the township. But she was not getting it because the officials said that she was not eligible for it as she had a ration card and that facility was only for those without the card. She said with the discontent that these officials think that if rice is given, it is enough, but that is not the case. Thinking of problems, she also mentioned she cannot buy sanitary napkins and have been using only cloth during menstruation to save money. She also said that she could not buy medicines without prescriptions as she does not have the money for going to a doctor.

She is living in her own house so she does not have the fear of eviction but she has spoken to people around her and she has not heard about evictions from anyone. From the PDS she only got rice but there was no provision of oil and pulses. She could not specify the amount.

She also said that the local village representatives did not cooperate to make her pension cards. Therefore, she is not getting the benefit. The money of the central government Jan-Dhan scheme has come in her account but since the bank is far away, crowded, and there is no ATM card, she has not been able to withdraw the money.

She said that the open government hospital was far away from her basti and the private hospital nearby was not open. She has access to soap and water but no masks, so she has started using handkerchiefs as masks instead.

The respondent was not happy with the work of the local authorities in her area, she said that in some areas, only some people have been given the task of distributing of rations, while the number of affected labourers is high, still, no relief has reached to them. The rule of social distance could not be maintained in the PDS shop; public knowledge awareness was not done properly. Bleaching powder was also not sprayed.

As immediate support, she said she needed cash support for buying the medicine and ration and getting her gas cylinder filled. As per suggestions for the government, she gave the following suggestions- (i) Pay attention to those who do not have pension cards; (ii) There should be some arrangement for burning stove to cook rice even for those who do not have

Ujjwala card. (ii) No one should sleep hungry, the government should work to fulfil the need for ration and medicine for those affected.

Case Study 3: Location: Kandhamal, Odisha

The respondent is a widow living in Kandhamal, Odisha. She did not know anything about the COVID-19 pandemic, she was only aware of the lockdown at the time of the interview. She said that the problem she has had during lockdown was that she is unable to go to collect firewood from the forest and grocery items from the shops outside her house due to the restriction on the movement.

As a single woman living alone, the respondent had a problem of accessing basic essential items such as grocery items, vegetables etc, and she is also physically not very strong, so she finds it difficult to manage everything on her own. She lives in her own house in the village so there is no fear of eviction for her. Most people in her village have their own houses, so she does not know of any eviction possibilities for anyone in her village. She said she has been receiving dry ration from the PDS but she could not give any detail about the amount. But she said that it was enough for her as she was the only person living by herself.

The respondent also mentioned that she has been receiving widow pension but since the bank is far away from her house, and there was no vehicle available, she has not been able to go and withdraw the money from the bank. That is the reason she has not been able to buy sanitation essentials like soaps from the shops in her village. She said there was a Primary Health Care (PHC) but it was not in the village, and she was not able to tell the distance of the PHC from her house. She had not needed to go to the PHC during the lockdown but she said even if she needs, she does not know if she will be able to go because of the unavailability of vehicles.

She said that she had not much idea of the panchayat's work during the pandemic in her area as she had not been going out of the house at all during the lockdown and interaction between the neighbours are also severely limited. She also said that the immediate support she needs is the provision of food items and sanitation essentials. And in the long run, she said that the government should focus on providing food support, health check-up and treatment for the elderly during the pandemic.

Case Study 4: Location: Bandipora, Jammu and Kashmir

The respondent is a 58 years old widow living with her four children. She is heading the family, having four children (2 girls & 2 boys), three are studying. The main challenges she is facing from last two months due to lockdown are financial problem, essential food supplies problem and impact on children mental health, not able to feed healthy food to her children, very difficult to earn a single penny due to lockdown. It is very difficult to get bread from the market due to lockdown nothing is available with shopkeepers. Other essential services products such as disinfectants and masks, it's very challenging and difficult to get access to them.

She also mentioned that she lives in her own house and does not have to worry about paying rent. She also said that she was receiving ration as per the government guidelines. As she had Antodaya Anna Yojana (AAY) category ration card so on time the ration is being distributed at PDS shops without any problem. She also said that she has been receiving widow pension, per month the government is disbursing 1000 rupees to her account. She was able to withdraw the amount from the nearest Khidmat Centre established by J&k Bank.

She said she does not have access to soap and sanitation essentials. She also said that there is one PHC in her village but it is not functioning as there are no doctors available there. She also expressed discontent over the performance of her panchayat in that area. She said that there is no work being done by the panchayat. She said that the immediate support she needed was financial support for purchasing of feed for livestock, essential supply for my family like Mustered oil, rice, Green Tea, soap, sanitizers etc.

The suggestions she had for the government were- (i) Hand cash Financial support to families; (ii) Distribution of essential supplies at doorsteps; (iii) Make arrangements for breaking the chain of COVID-19 pandemic.

Major Findings from Case Studies

The major issues emerging from these case studies are-

(i) The lack of awareness about COVID-19 among the older single women living on their own which needs to be corrected as the elderly population is more vulnerable to the disease and lack of proper awareness among them can lead to the higher number of cases and deaths due to COVID-19

(ii) There is a huge lack of awareness about social security benefits available for women in India from the state as well as the central government. Due to that reason, many single women are deprived of their deserved benefits.

(iii) The lack of action and initiative on the part of local administration in making the benefits of these schemes available to the single women of their area of work is a problem for rural women as mentioned in the second case study.

(iv) There is sheer unavailability of care support for single women living alone. Single women are often stigmatized and have no support system to help them. In times like this pandemic, when the interaction with the community becomes severely limited, it becomes even more difficult for single women without the presence of any support system.

(v) The loss of livelihood for self-employed single women or single women engaged in informal sector work is a problem that has come out in all the case studies and is related to the other issues that have emerged. With the lack of awareness about benefit schemes, they face financial difficulties in times like this when their regular source of income has halted. With rural women, the scope of finding an alternate source of income becomes even more difficult and the inefficiency of the local authorities in helping them avail the benefits of social security schemes makes situations even more bizarre for single women from rural India.

(vi) Inability to access services like banking or hospitals due to the unavailability of transportation facilities is another important issue. There should be doorstep delivery of cash support and essential items for women and all eligible women must be registered for the social security benefit schemes to help them avail additional support during the pandemic.

Recommendations

The recommendations, based on above findings, are as follows:

(i) Awareness generation to reduce the stigma around single women should be one of the areas that the local governance at village level and Civil Society Organisations should work along with the participation of the village community. This is an important aspect for ensuring a safe environment for single women.

(ii) Increasing awareness generation on COVID-19 for older single women as they are more vulnerable to the disease. A village-level cohort of volunteers should be trained to ensure that a campaign with special focus on single women (especially the elderly people) should be initiated at the Panchayat level. A register that records all the single women should be maintained at Panchayat level and door to door awareness campaign should be organised to ensure hundred percent reach out.

(iii) The above-mentioned cohort of volunteers should also visit each of the single women houses and make them aware of the different government schemes for single women such as Widow pension, Deserted Women Pension etc. A large section of the single women from the rural areas are either illiterate or just know enough to sign their names. They cannot read the pamphlets or wall writings or hoardings which talks about government schemes. They are also economically not strong enough to have smartphones or televisions which has become an effective medium of information dissemination nowadays. Hence the door to door awareness campaign will help them to get the information. These volunteers should also help them to access the benefits of the schemes and get necessary documentation for the same.

(iv) The local authority while distributing relief or rehabilitation materials should increase their focus to include single women. Most of the single women are living from hand to mouth. Hence in the priority category, the Panchayat should ensure that all the single women should be included in the beneficiary list. Provision of cash support and essential items support for single women during the pandemic should be the priority for the panchayats.

(v) In many cases of single women who do not have their own home and stay in the rented accommodation or with relatives, they should be protected from eviction due to non-payment of rent in the pandemic.

(vi) Doorstep market linkage for disabled farmers, livestock rearers, craftsmen and artisans for selling their produce and products when they cannot go to market due to unavailability of vehicles.

(vii) This is an opportunity for local administration to strengthen the livelihood of the single women and support them to initiate resilient livelihood options.

viii) The Central, State and District, as well as the local government, should not look at the problems of women from one perspective. They need to understand that women are not a homogeneous group. Hence a special programme for single women should be framed to ensure their safe lives and resilient livelihood.

Conclusion

The outbreak of the pandemic has shown the already existing glaring inequalities in our societies. In this patriarchal world, women are undoubtedly the most marginalised community, but women are not a homogeneous group. Single women are one of the most neglected and vulnerable groups among the larger community of women. These vulnerabilities are seen in all spheres through this case studies like access to health care, jobs and employment, wage parity and even access to basic services like sanitation. This situation has also laid bare open the unpreparedness of most countries including the developed ones to deal with it. It has displayed fundamental weakness in our basic structures that have exposed prevailing poverty, fragile health systems, lack of holistic education systems, failing social protection systems, etc.

References

CSW64 / Beijing+25 (2020) | Commission on the Status of Women | UN Women – Headquarters. (n.d.). Retrieved August 5, 2020, from https://www.unwomen.org/en/csw/csw64-2020

The Pandemic Exposes India's Apathy Toward Migrant Workers - The Atlantic. (n.d.). Retrieved August 5, 2020, from https://www.theatlantic.com/ideas/archive/2020/04/the-pandemic-exposes-indias-two-worlds/609838/

Why the lockdown is harder on single women - Times of India. (n.d.). Retrieved August 9, 2020, from https://timesofindia.indiatimes.com/india/labour-of-life-in-lockdown-taking-toll-on-urban-single-women/articleshow/75292546.cms

Chapter - 4

Impact of COVID-19 on Indian Migrant Workers in the Gulf Countries

— Dr. Trilok Chandan Goud

Introduction

Migration of Indian migrant workers to West Asia (Gulf Countries) started in the 1970s and peaked up in the early 1980s (Prakash 1998; Goud 2020), the destination countries of the Gulf region are Saudi Arabia, UAE, Kuwait, Oman, Bahrain, and Qatar (Azeez and Begum 2009; Hussain 2016; MEA 2020). All these six countries called as GCC (Gulf Cooperation Council) countries have similar policies regarding the migrant workers.

The global price hike of petroleum and oil products in the early 1970s changed the socio-economic scenario of the Gulf countries (Khadria 2006; Pradhan 2010). Large revenues increased the process of industrialization, infrastructure development, and social change in the six GCC countries characterized by massive investment in social and economic growth necessitating the service of a large number of foreign workers. However, development required the service of a large number of foreign workers, as the GCC countries could not provide the native labor supplies. The foreign workers met these challenges of labor shortage who mostly came from South Asian countries such as India, Nepal, Sri Lanka, Bangladesh, Pakistan, and the Philippines for working in construction sites, construction allied services, oil companies, retail and service sectors (Nurses, teachers, doctors, and engineers) (Jain 2007). Among the South Asian countries, India continues to be the largest contributor for sending migrant workers. For decades, Indian migrant workers have played an important role in building the economies of the Gulf countries, providing manpower for the key construction, retail, hospitality, tourism, and travel sectors.

Methodology

This chapter is mainly based on secondary and primary data collected from various national and international documents such as MEA, IOM and ILO. The basic methods used for collecting information for this chapter were telephonic interviews with migrant workers in the Gulf and returnees from the Gulf and migrant rights activists in India. Apart from interviews, we reviewed different research papers and news items which are published in the news papers. This chapter in not an ethnographic study primarily focused on the literary sources.

Migration to the Gulf

Migration to Gulf countries is mainly unskilled and semi-skilled laborers for working as manual laborers and domestic workers (house maids). It is oriented towards labor and service occupations on a contract basis, more than 8.9 million Indian migrants live in Gulf countries, with most of them coming from Kerala, Tamil Nadu, Andhra Pradesh, Telangana, Uttar Pradesh, Bihar, Rajasthan and Punjab (MEA, 2020)[1]. Migration to Gulf countries started as laborers in oil industries and later stage as construction workers, domestic workers (housemaids), and in other service occupations.

Graph 1: The number of persons emigrated with Emigration Clearance Required (ECR) Certificate from Selected States During the year 2018.

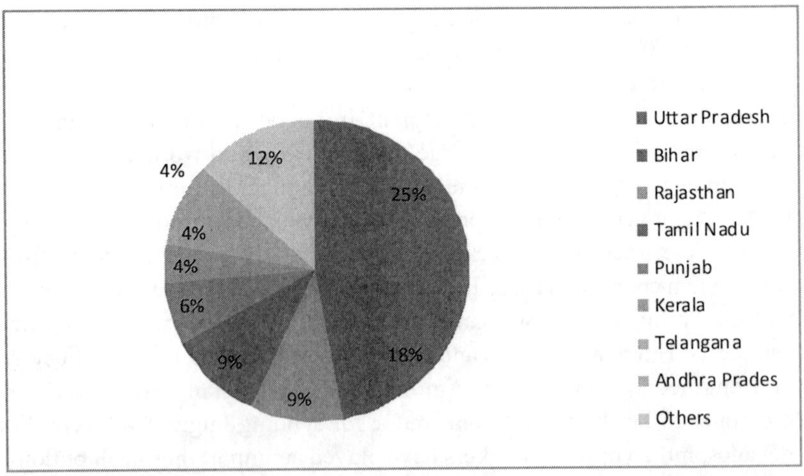

Source: Compiled from Ministry of External Affairs Annual report 2018-2019.

For a brief period during the 1990-91 Gulf War (Iraq-Kuwait war), the number of Indian workers in the Gulf had to leave countries due to Indian

Table 1: Estimates of Indian migrants in GCC Countries 1975-2019.

Years	*Bahrain*	*Kuwait*	*Oman*	*Qatar*	*Saudi Arabia*	*UAE*
1975	17,250	32,105	38,500	27,800	34,500	107,500
1979	26,000	65,000	60,000	30,000	100,000	152,000
1983	30,000	115,000	100,000	40,000	270,000	250,000
1987	77,000	100,000	184,000	50,000	380,000	225,000
1991	100,000	88,000	220,000	75,000	600,000	400,000
2004	150,000	400,000	450,000	150,000	1,500,000	1,000,000
2008	230,000	550,000	600,000	220,000	1,600,000	1,200,000
2012	350,000	579,390	718,642	500,000	1,789,000	1,750,000
2016	295,504	880,567	795,082	630,000	2,960,000	2,600,000
2018	312,918	928,421	688,226	691,539	2,812,408	3,100,000
2019	326,658	1,029,861	781,141	746,550	2,594,947	3,425,144

Source: Jain (2007) & compiled from MEA Reports (2001, 2016, 2018, 2019.

government restrictions. However, when the situation normalized the emigration from India had again picked up as the demand for labor in the GCC countries increased and diversified across many sectors from construction to services sector, tourism, retail business, oil and manufacturing sector, etc. In 2020, the expected total stock of Indian migrants in the Gulf countries is estimated at 8.9 million (MEA[4], 2020).

Reasons for Migration

Indian migrants in the early stage were mostly those who have low agricultural land and some of them are even landless. Even those having agricultural land are unable to cultivate and seek profits due to droughts and low irrigation facilities. Apart from this, natural calamities like famines and floods, shrinking of the cottage industry, and lack of employment opportunities forced many of them to migrate to urban areas and to migrate to the Gulf countries (Bhat and Sahoo, 2005). Because of the shrinking of cottage industries and traditional caste occupations, many backward caste/communities (especially the youth) lost their livelihood and this has compelled them to search for new occupations, these migrants are mostly from rural areas.

The process of emigration plays a crucial role because most of the migrants emigrate through private recruiting agencies and those agencies make fraud by taking money from the migrants, they provide tourist/travel visa to the migrants and send them to host countries, and they are undocumented (Irregular) migrants. Informal, family, and personal networks are also a major source for getting visas and work permits; the job category also depends on the networks. Sub-agents (Unauthorized agents) in the rural areas are the crucial players in sending migrants to the Gulf countries. A large number of migrants depend on sub-agents for getting visas and work permits, these sub-agents charge huge visa fees from the prospective migrants.

The majority of the migrants who are recruited to the Gulf have incurred costs to undertake that migration; most of them take debt from moneylenders and pay huge fees to the recruiting agents. The agents are more concerned about their commissions – because of competition among the agents – some lured the potential migrants to arrange those well-paid jobs in the Gulf countries with attractive income.

Non-payment and late payment of wages and salaries is a common complaint of migrant workers in the GCC countries. Most migrant workers in GCC countries come from rural areas and work in low-paid jobs in construction, hospitality, and domestic work as maids, security guards, and drivers. Many people take out loans to migrate, which trap them for several years in cycles of debt and exploitation.

Poverty, on the one hand, unemployment on the other hand, with huge financial burden most of the Indian migrants are working for low skilled and low paid jobs. Although these migrants are low paid workers in the Gulf, India is receiving huge remittances from the Gulf because these migrants often work on a temporary work on contract and remit most of their earnings to home.

India received the highest amount of remittances from Gulf countries, the policies of the Gulf countries indirectly helped the workers to send remittances back home, and the Gulf countries do not allow foreign workers to purchase immovable property in those countries. The amount gained as salaries by the workers is sent to their families/homes (Goud, 2020). Remittances play a bigger role in improving family well-being among the poorer and more disadvantaged groups (Mahapatro et al. 2015). According to Kerala Migration Survey the estimated total remittances to Kerala are rupees 85,092 crore in 2018 (Rajan and Zachariah 2020).

According to the World Bank report (2019) in the year 2018, India is the highest recipient of remittances at $79 billion and most of the remittances are from the Gulf region. Migration always delivers major economic benefits to home countries; migrants send money to support families back home. In crisis situation like COVID-19 there maybe decline in the remittances.

Impact of COIVD-19 on the Gulf Migrants

Most of the migrants are from the states of Uttar Pradesh, Bihar, Kerala, Tamil Nadu, Andhra Pradesh, Telangana, Rajasthan, Punjab, and West Bengal. Today, their condition has become questionable due to the COVID-19 pandemic.

Table 2: State-wise figures of emigration clearance endorsements, 2007-2014.

State	*2007*	*2008*	*2009*	*2010*	*2011*	*2012*	*2013*	*2014*
Andhra Pradesh	1,05,044	97,530	69,233	72,220	71,589	92,803	1,03,049	53,104
Karnataka	27,014	22,413	18,565	17,295	15,394	17,960	17,798	15,054
Kerala	1,50,475	1,80,703	1,19,384	1,04,101	86,783	98,178	85,909	66,058
Punjab	53,942	54,469	27,291	30,974	31,866	37,472	48,836	48,431
Rajasthan	70,896	64,601	44,744	47,803	42,239	50,295	41,676	48,123
Tamil Nadu	1,50,842	1,28,791	78,841	84,510	68,732	78,185	83,087	83,202
Uttar Pradesh	91,613	1,39,254	1,25,783	1,40,826	1,55,301	191,341	2,18,292	2,29,444
Telangana	0	0	0	0	0	0	0	38,531
Total	8,09,453	8,48,601	6,10,272	6,41,356	6,26,565	7,47,041	8,16,655	8,04,878

Source: Data compiled from POE Analytics and MOIA Annual Reports 2005-2014.

As per the above table, it shows the majority of the migrants belong to the Kerala followed by Tamil Nadu and Andhra Pradesh. There has been a steady decline in Kerala's contribution to Gulf migration since 1998, but at the same time, the shares of Tamil Nadu and Andhra Pradesh have increased by considerable numbers. One of the reasons for the decline in labor migration from Kerala during 1998-2004 is that larger numbers of people migrating from Kerala are graduates, who are engaged in skilled and professional related activities in the Gulf. These categories of migrants do not require emigration clearance;[5] whereas the majority of migrants from Tamil Nadu and Andhra Pradesh (Telangana) require emigration clearance to migrate to foreign countries, as they are mainly unskilled workers (Azeez and Begum, 2009).

There is a high increase in migration from Uttar Pradesh in recent years. In 2014, Uttar Pradesh became the top state with 229,444 migrants, followed by Bihar with 98,721 persons and Andhra Pradesh with 91,635 persons (MEA, 2015). Pertinently, while Uttar Pradesh and Bihar replaced positions of Kerala and Tamil Nadu. In 2019, Uttar Pradesh continued with top position followed by Bihar and Rajasthan with third position (MEA, 2020).

Table 3: Number of Persons from Top Eight States Obtained Emigration Clearance in the year 2019

State	*Number of Persons*
Uttar Pradesh	116,251
Bihar	55,423
Rajasthan	28,982
Tamil Nadu	27,783
Kerala	19,173
Andhra Pradesh	18,005
Punjab	14,665
Telangana	13,388

Source: Ministry of External Affairs Annual Report 2020.

Note: These are the top eight sending states to the Gulf countries.

The slowdown in oil prices and the economic recession along with the corona (COVID-19) effect is hurting Gulf companies all at once. Companies in the Gulf have been forced to close due to continued self-restraint. As discussed, the majority of the migrant workers working in the Gulf are small and middle-income persons. They all work as contract workers in different service sectors. Along with them, many migrants work as daily wage workers. Similarly, a large number of migrants who migrated to the Gulf and they work on tourist visas illegally are mostly from India.

Lockdown and Social/Physical Distancing

In the early stage of the pandemic around 2,061 Indians tested positive only in the Gulf countries (The Hindu, April 16, 2020). Due to the COVID-19 pandemic, GCC countries imposed lockdown to control the pandemic, this compelled many sectors to shutdown their economic activities and it affected the lives of the migrant workers. Stranded workers faced difficulties in the host nations without jobs, money, and sufficient food. Living and working conditions of the Gulf migrant workers are very difficult to maintain social/physical distance, a large number of the construction workers live in labor camps with 10-15 persons in a single room, and many other migrants share their accommodation with fellow migrants in rented houses. Accommodation is a major problem for many migrant workers, due to costly rents; they share accommodation with 10-12 persons in a single room. Poor hygiene is a serious concern for these migrant workers.

In the situation of COVID-19 pandemic, migrant workers, especially those who are undocumented (Illegal), stood out as among the sectors most vulnerable to exclusion, social stigma, and discrimination, health care is a serious issue for the undocumented migrants. Migrant workers in the countries of destination in GCC have lost their income to support themselves and their families due to the unexpected business closures and lockdowns. Migrants with COVID-19 positive are emotionally disturbed by the fact that their health is declining, visa expiration, and closure of many companies have made more and more difficult for them to sustain.

Further, many migrant workers who have completed their employment contracts or have been terminated from work are stranded without adequate food, shelter, and means of returning to India. Even those who were fortunate enough to have been able to return to their own countries of origin still face stigma, discrimination, and exclusion even from their fellow villagers due to fear of the corona pandemic.

In this backdrop, that the Government of India has taken the initiative to bring the migrant workers back to their places, with a mission called 'Vande Bharat', but 14 days quarantine is a big problem for many Gulf returnees, although these low-paid migrants have to pay for the air tickets and they have to pay the quarantine fee. Over 300,000 Indians register to return from Gulf region (Hindustantimes, May 05, 2020).

Return, Rehabilitation, and Re-integration

In the Corona (COVID-19) crisis, the most vulnerable section of the people are migrant workers, they may be Internal, Inter-state or International migrants. Now it is impossible to imagine what the situation would be like if those workers returned to native place. Due to the decline in oil prices and COIVD-19 impact, economic activities in the Gulf countries are going to affect for a while, we cannot assume how long it takes to resume the economic activities, and the majority of the migrants will not find jobs for a period. A large number of migrants prefer to return to their home country and some are in dilemma to return or stay back.

The return of the migrant workers is a big challenge for our home country. Most of the workers who were recruited to the Gulf would have incurred costs to undertake that migration. Workers paid a huge amount of money to recruitment agencies for obtaining visas and work permits. They are often paid by taking a loan from moneylenders, at high-interest rates. Migrants regularly send remittances, which would have paid towards repaying the debt/loan. In this present condition, they are unable to send the remittances back home, if they return home they have to clear the loans and provide money for the family livelihood.

These poor low-skilled and low paid workers migrate to support their families and remit their all earnings. Consequently, on the distress return, they encounter a difficult economic situation at home. Unemployment in the rural areas is the major reason for the migrant workers to migrate to a foreign nation, if they return in the distress, how they will cope-up and find employment?

Similarly, re-integration for returnees becomes a serious problem, as they undergo social, economic, and psychological pressure when they are burdened with debt. The majority of migrants had taken personal loans with a huge interest amount on it so the amount increased. The amount earned in the Gulf was so meager that all their savings and remittances were used to pay off the interest, leave alone to clear the basic amount of loan.

In 2008-2009, the global financial crisis caused great depression among the Gulf migrant workers in Telugu states; due to job loss, many victims committed suicide in depression. This is the time to act in a positive way to protect the migrants with proactive measures in the post-COVID-19 scenario.

Recommendations

So it is time for our governments to plan for them an employment opportunity. Different policies and programs have to be implemented through reunification for migrant workers who return. If governments make efforts towards that, workers have a better future. If we fail to support the migrant workers both internally and internationally, the future of these people will be questionable.

The Government and NGO's should give moral support to the returnees and encourage them to start a new life; the Government should also safeguard the returnees against discrimination. Discrimination against migrant workers are always high in both host and home societies, we have to ensure that discrimination does not increase and lead to social tension and conflict. The government should take responsibility for return, rehabilitation, and reintegration. It's high time to respond to the Global Compact for Migration and its objectives which we should safeguard human rights of all migrants, social inclusion, cohesion, and all forms of discrimination, including gender, xenophobia, and intolerance. The government shall have international cooperation and governance of migration in all its dimensions, including at borders, on its transit, entry, return, readmission, integration, and reintegration. Effective social protection systems are important to safeguarding the deprived and vulnerable migrants during this crisis at home and destination. Following measures are recommended for improving the condition of migrants who returned from Gulf countries:

(i) There shall be special funds available to provide financial assistance to Gulf returnees who are in distress.

(ii) Interest-free loans shall be given to the returnees.

(iii) They need to be encouraged and supported in setting up of small-scale industries.

(iv) Skill training through institutes like NIRD&PR, RSETI, SVEP for self-employment need to be provided.

(v) Strong bilateral agreements/understanding with host nations are required to protect and safeguard stranded migrants.

(vi) All support to stranded migrants and their access to healthcare, food, accommodation, and transport need to be provided through the Indian Embassies in host countries.

(vii) Government of India should arrange free air tickets for the distressed migrants to return home.

(viii) The government shall support the families of deceased migrants.

Conclusion

Different projects and studies on the Gulf migration in India analyzed large scale migration is happening from rural areas due to low-employment opportunities and failure in agriculture. They are mostly low educated and low paid workers; migrants in the Gulf countries always face several problems like low standard of living, delay in salary payment, harsh working conditions. Women work as domestic workers in local Arab houses and some face problems like sexual harassment and ill-treatment by owners.

Due to COIVD-19 pandemic the companies in the Gulf region are affected with huge economic loss and it showed adverse impact on the migrant workers. Many migrant workers are stranded without jobs and money; Indian government repatriated some persons with a mission called 'Vande Bharat' and some are still waiting to return. Majority of the Indian migrant workers are from rural areas and they migrated to the Gulf due to unemployment at their native places. Large number of them incurred money for the process of migration and job, if they return in the middle it will be a big loss for them and it shows adverse impact on the rural economy. As discussed we need to take measures to protect the migrants who return and also who are stranded in the host nation.

References

Azeez, A. and Begum, M. (2009). Gulf Migration, Remittances and Economic impact. *Journal of Social Sciences*, 20 (1): 55-60.

Bhat, C., and Sahoo, A.K. (2005). Transnational Networks of Indian Diasporic Communities: The Case of Telugu Diaspora. *Man in India*, Vol. 85, No. 1&2.

Goud, T. C. (2020). Indian Immigrants in the Gulf Countries: Issues, Trends and Polices. In Sahoo. A.K and Rao P. V (Eds) *Indian Diaspora and Transnationalism: Trends and Issues in the 21st century*. (pp.239-260). New Delhi :Serials Publications.

Hussian, Z. (2016). GCC's immigration policy in the post 1990s: Contextualising South Asian migration. In Jain, P.C and Oommen, G. Z. (Eds). *South Asian Migration to Gulf Countries: History, Policies, Development*. New York: Routledge.

Jain, P. C. (2007). Indian Diaspora in West Asia: A Reader. New Delhi: Manohar Publications.

Khadria, B. (2006). *India: Skilled Migration to Developed Countries, Labour Migration to the Gulf.* Asia Research Institute: National University of Singapore.

Mahapatro, S., A.Bailey, K.S.James and I. Hutter. (2015). Remittances and Household Expenditure Patterns in India and Selected States. *Migration and Development, Vol 6(1): 3-101.*

Prakash, B. A. (1998). Gulf Migration and its Economic Impact: The Kerala Experience. *Economic and Political Weekly*, Vol.33, No.50: 3209 to 3213.

Pradhan, S. (2010). India and the Gulf Cooperation Council (GCC): An Economic and Political Perspective. *Strategic Analysis*, 3 (1): 93-103.

Rajan, S.I. and Zachariah. K.C. (2020). New Evidences from the Kerala Migration Survey, 2018. Economic and Political Weekly, Vol. 55, No: 4. Special Article.

[1] http://mea.gov.in/images/attach/NRIs-and-PIOs_1.pdf).

[2] ECR- Emigration clearance required

[3] http://www.mea.gov.in/Uploads/PublicationDocs/31719_MEA_AR18_19.pdf

[4] Ministry of External Affairs

[5] Emigration Act, 1983 provides that no citizen of India shall migrate unless he obtains emigration clearance from Protector of Emigrants.

Chapter - 5

Role Played by Self Help Groups in Combating COVID-19 in Odisha

— *Dr. Biswa Mohana Jena,*
Dr. Binita Nanda

Introduction

The Self Help Group movement of India has originated from insignificant savings and credit groups that support to development of underprivileged rural women into the world's biggest international boards of the poor. Presently, around 67 million women in India are members of six million SHGs. They have been assigned the responsibility and actively participated in creating awareness on COVID -19 at the community level as much as possible, concentrating mostly on women those who have little awareness on hygiene and sanitation. They circulated pamphlets targeting rural areas and urban areas also, mostly women. From delivering ration to setting up vegetable shops, and making people understand the necessity of remaining indoors during lockdown, around 70 lakh women members are actively shouldering vital responsibilities across Odisha.

A contagion is not new to the human history. But what makes the COVID-19 contagion special is that it takes place in an unparalleled backdrop when the inter-dependence and interconnectivity among people, among different countries and continents started developing. The achievements that people around the world have made in intelligence, technology as well as transportation, have made them both psychologically as well as physically interdependent globally. The danger of spread in rural regions is quite high. This is because of various components, including absence of mindfulness, a constrained flexibly of clean water, low degrees of sustenance, and in particular, unprepared and inadequate general wellbeing communities and region medical clinics. In any case, with perpetually scant assets and an absence of subsidizing, numerous NGOs are not, at this point ready to give backing to SHGs. Thus, the less-settled SHGs are deteriorating. Accordingly, government or development organisations like the National Bank for Agriculture and Rural Development could help support and fortify SHGs by combining them and helping them get to the financing they have to build their effectively noteworthy effect on rustic jobs.

The Chief Minister of Odisha, Shri Naveen Pattnaik had in recent times said that it was encouraging to see an outstanding response of women, especially the members of Self- Help Groups, during the critical time. Moreover, Shri Dharmendra Pradhan, the Union Petroleum Minister has also poured applauses on the various SHGs. He recently has tweeted that the nari shakti (Women empowerment) in Odisha is working enormously to drag the state out of the Corona well.

Almost immediately after the nationwide lockdown was imposed to contain the spread of the deadly Coronavirus, the members of the women SHGs came forward to feed and help the deprived section. Above eight thousand SHGs are recently engaged in this task. Mrs. Sujata R. Karthikeyan, Director of Mission Shakti has been coordinating the efforts of the women SHGs. The complete health service tool is being supported by thousands of doctors and nurses. While doctors and nurses are unswervingly handling the patients, thousands of ancillary nurse mid-wives (ANMs), Anganwadi as well as ASHA workers are going door to doorin order to check peoples' health. Besides, the members of Gruhalaxmi Cooperative Self Help Group (GCSHG) of Dhenkanal district are preparing face masks and shields to combat the virus from scattering. Approximately, twenty women of the SHG from three neighbouring villages of Kurunti Nuagaon and Asanbani under Hindol block are engaged making face masks. Again, President Sabita Nayak of Narendrapur village Gruhalaxmi Cooperative Self Help Group, said that they were not able to meet the need of face mask and are still trying to help people with support from Tata Steel. According to Russell, Self-help groups are small group of members having membership of 10 to 15 members who work together for their livelihood through financing by banks, NGOs and micro finance institutions. They are often run by women and studies indicate it leads to women empowerment.

JEEVIKA in Bihar has started giving awareness pamphlets during corona virus pandemic. JEEVIKA is trying to reach 1.4 lakhs SHGs and make people aware of the pandemic consequences and take precaution not to fall in its prey by providing masks, gloves, ration and sanitizer. Community awareness through announcement in mobile vans.

In Tamil Naidu, SHGs volunteers are playing a vital role in ensuring public health, distribution of PDS, gloves, sanitizers and maintain social distancing norms.

In the above context, the present study attempts to understand the role played by SHGs in combating COVID-19 particulary in meeting gaps in demand and availability of face masks, hand sanitizers and protective equipment; combating misinformation, spreading right awareness; and providing banking and financial solutions to rural communities. The study also analyses issues and challenges faced by SHGs and makes recommendations to further improve their effectiveness in combating spread of COVID-19 and making lives of affected rural communities easier.

Role of SHGs in Combating COVID-19

SHGs takes four to five years to arrive at the phase of self-maintainability, moving on from utilization and low beneficial exercises to monetary undertakings. Be that as it may, a portion of the SHG individuals may not attempt enterprise because of absence of inspiration, suitable business openings, administrative abilities, specialized skill, esteem expansion to their items or administrations, monetary proficiency, satisfactory flexibly of credit, showcase linkages, and so on. In addition, the SHGs are burdened with non-revolution of authority positions, lacking hand-holding backing of Self-Help Promoting Institutions (SHPIs) and change in the administration's approach.

The infection COVID-19 has changed the whole world. To alleviate the immense misfortune a milestone model has been started, which is explicitly called the Self-Help Group Bank Linkage Program (SHG-BLP) by the National Bank for Agriculture and Rural Development (NABARD) in 1992. The principle point is to give sensible doorstep banking administrations as a major aspect of money related incorporation drive in India. Today, the SHG-BLP is viewed as the biggest small scale fund program on the planet with an all-out enrolment of 100.14 lakh gatherings (covering almost 12 crore families) across India and having expanded guarantee free credits of 87,098 crore to 50.77 lakh SHGs as on March 31, 2020. It is fascinating to take note of that more than 92 percent of the SHG individuals are ladies.

SHGs have risen as edge labourers and the last mile associate among governments and the individuals during this emergency. SHG ladies are performing a significant role in response to COVID-19. They are making face covers, hand sanitizers, PPE packs, circulating bring home proportion, scattering COVID-19 related data and running network kitchens to take care of the vulnerable. The job of SHGs has never been a higher priority than now and can end up being an uncommon silver covering in the pain that SHGs are managing. Ladies can approach and take initiative and advancement jobs in their towns. It is an open door that the SHG development must profit by.

Going ahead, it will be critical to reinforce the development, to ensure it can assimilate the monetary, social and wellbeing of community during this emergency. Post the lockdown governments ought to assess, the speculation by SHG development into COVID-19 reaction and its effect on the SHG economy. It would likewise be helpful to have clear rules from the specialists, about when and how SHGs can reconvene and what insurances they should take at the same time. SHGs ought to likewise use computerized stages, to guarantee the progression of right data, to stay in touch with one another and with the change of preparing instructional methods, to convey specific sorts of trainings. While the advanced stages can't fill in for week after week gatherings, it goes some path in offering a brief answer for the prompt issue.

During circumstances such as the present when correspondence through innovation denotes another type of solidarity, we should use the current methods available to us and find new and imaginative approaches to advance; so we don't lose the force picked up in the SHG development in the course of the most recent 30 years. Despite the fact that the Coronavirus has tossed numerous difficulties to the individuals from SHGs with respect to directing physical gathering, preparing investment funds (physical money notes) of the gathering, pivoting the cash for interior loaning among the individuals, keeping the physical money towards reimbursement of advances, and keeping up printed copy of records, computerized channels, nonetheless, made their life basic.

Figure 1 represents the number of SHGs involved in producing face masks in different states of India as on March 2020. The total of SHGs in the country stands at 14,522, including 25 states. The number of SHGs in Odisha State stands at 202, which is more than 10 states viz., Haryana, Himachal Pradesh, Jharkhand, Karnataka, Mizoram, Nagaland, Puducherry, Sikkim, Tripura and Uttarakhand. Besides, it is represented in the graph that Andhra Pradesh has the highest number of SHGs, followed by Tamil Nadu, Madhya Pradesh and Rajasthan.

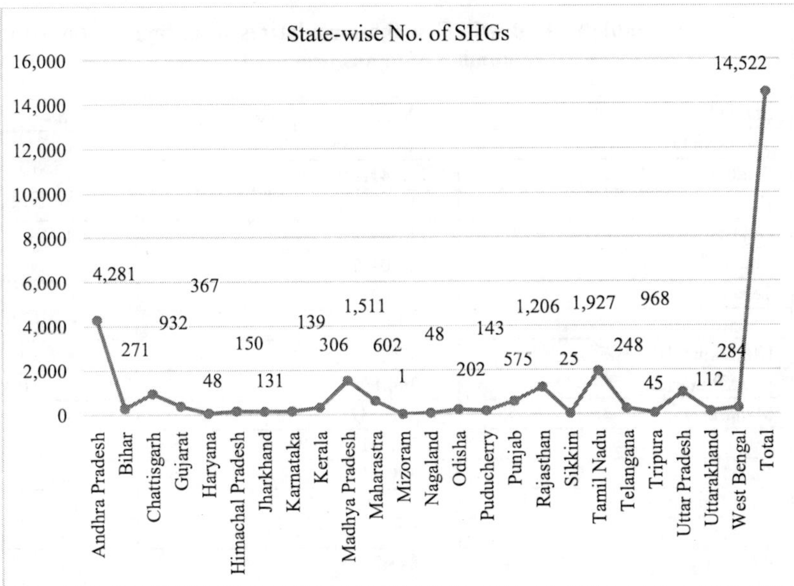

Source- Business today

Figure-1: Graph representing the number of SHGs involved in producing face-masks in different states of India as on March 2020.

Issues and Challenges Faced by SHGs

The Non Performing Assets (NPAs) of the SHG-BLP flooded from . 423 crore in 2007-08 to 4,524 crore in 2018-19. NPAs arrived at a pinnacle level of 7.40 percent in the Financial Year (FY) 2014-15 and later tumbled to 5.19 percent as on March 31, 2019. The circumstance of terrible advances has made further more chances turning out to be issue. There are numerous difficulties to the individuals SHGs as for physical gathering, activating investment funds, pivot of the cash, money reimbursement of advances, computerized channels, and keeping up printed version of records, anyway made their life basic. They can keep up their records in e-Shakti (an advanced activity of NABARD for keeping up SHGs' books of records, along these lines improving their financial assessment).

The individuals from self improvement gatherings (SHGs) in various towns the nation over have bolstered in delivering face veils in a major number to meet the unexpected prerequisite. Well beyond 132 lakh face veils have at this point been created by the individuals from numerous SHGs under the Ministry of Rural Development's National Rural Livelihood Mission (MRD-NRLM).

Table 1- Rank-wise distribution of states according to number of masks produced

States	*No. of Masks produced*	*Rank*
Tamil Nadu	2,601,735	1
Andhra Pradesh	2,541,440	2
Kerala	1,577,770	3
Gujarat	1,049,319	4
Madhya Pradesh	1,004,419	5
Telangana	580,000	6
Chhattisgarh	549,712	7
Uttarakhand	474,490	8
Uttar Pradesh	364,894	9
Maharashtra	362,332	10
Bihar	349,517	11
Jharkhand	300,215	12
West Bengal	291,794	13
Odisha	278,076	14
Punjab	243,268	15
Karnataka	156,155	16
Haryana	146,800	17
Puducherry	120,380	18
Himachal Pradesh	100,000	19
Rajasthan	92,890	20
Sikkim	10,000	21
Nagaland	6,819	22
Tripura	4,650	23
Mizoram	100	24

Source: Ministry of Rural Development's National Rural Livelihood Mission.

In the course of the most recent couple of days, the individuals from a sum of 14,522 SHGs in twenty four states covering over 399 regions of the nation are powerfully associated with the creation of face masks. While in five regions of Andhra Pradesh, 21,028 individuals from 4,281 SHGs created 25,41,440 and 10,780 individuals from 1,927 SHGs in 32 areas of Tamil Nadu delivered 26,01,735 covers. The individuals from SHGs (Refer Figure 2) of different states, for example, Bihar, Chhattisgarh, Kerala, Gujarat, Haryana, Madhya Pradesh, Uttar Pradesh and numerous North Eastern states in the nation are additionally effectively associated with delivering face covers. Summarizing, a sum of 65,936 SHG individuals from 14,522 SHGs are effectively drawn in and have made 132 lakh face veils. From the Table 1, it is indicated that among all the States in India, Odisha remains at fourteenth position in creation and delivering a sum of 278,076 face covers.

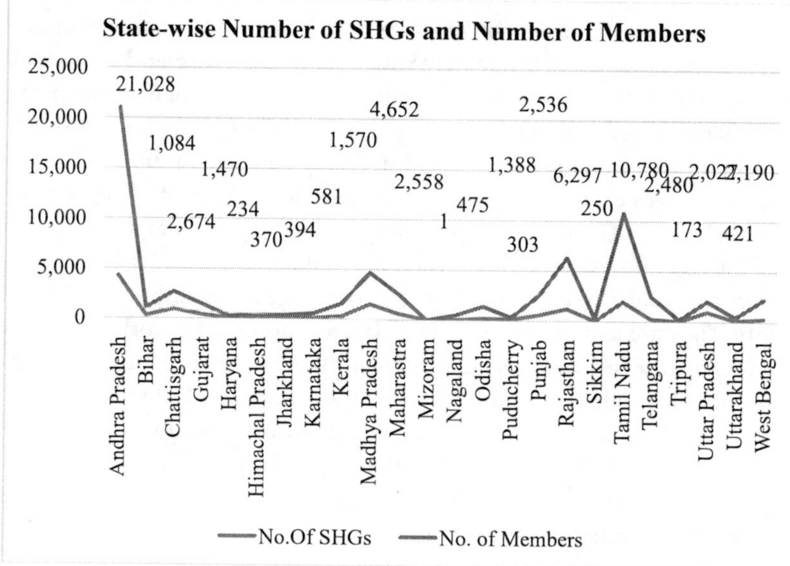

Figure 2: Graph Representing Number of Members in SHGs in Different States in India

Recommendations

SHGs are presently producing masks that can be worn, and the ASHA, SHG Workers are spreading information among network individuals. Also, some Civil Society Organisations, for example, PRADAN, have created and are dispersing Information, Education, and Communication (IEC) material, and making people aware through SHGs. Hindered monetary movement in urban regions affects rural areas also. Various investigations and experience from the field demonstrate that a noteworthy extent of rustic family unit livelihoods originates from movement and daily wage workers. The casual business in urban areas being seriously influenced has brought about loss of rural income. Furthermore, gigantic cutbacks and absence of alleviation measures are pushing transients to come back to their towns, which would expand the danger of the spread of the infection. However, the consequence that the pandemic brought is that complications in one country will turn out to be global ones. Near about 70 lakh women members of MISSION SHAKITI SHG of Odisha are working day and night to help the people during COVID19. They have been helping people to provide basic amenities of the Government like dry ration, vegetables, groceries, cooked food through community kitchen. Near about 45000 people are been given free food through Community Kitchen under MISSION SHAKTI.

The concept of stay home and stay safe is been advertised regularly among all households of the society with a view to get essential goods and services at their droop steps or close to them. SHGs, throughout the country, helps all to maintain the social distancing norms. These include production of ready to eat take home ration and doorstep delivery of dry ration and fresh vegetables as well as other hygiene products. Concept of vegetables on wheels of SHGs are providing solution to many problems. They are reaching to children, school students, pregnant women, target group and vulnerable groups. SHG members are also engaged in distribution of PDS supply. They are taking the risk of their life and doing their work as corona warriors, getting infected also during their duty. So it a recommended that they should be alert and take safety precautions by following social distancing norms during their work. They are also engaged in distribution of study materials to the school children, promoting the safe hygiene practices in every community with a view to fight COVID-19 with honesty, hard work, dedication and devotion.

More than 7000 SHGs are working daily, 5247 Gram Panchayat level free kitchen have been advocated with local bodies for the betterment of village people. Cooked meals to near about 3.27 lakhs people have been served. In particular, the SHG individuals can use digital mediums for monetary transactions; they can meet their companions through social/ advanced media without meeting face to face; they can keep up their records in e-Shakti (an advanced activity of NABARD for keeping up SHGs' books of records, consequently improving their FICO rating). Likewise, the SHG individuals ought to be given adaptability in reimbursement of bank advances — for example, rather than daily, weekly reimbursement plan be followed. In this way, there exists an open door for SHG ladies to make face masksveils, sanitisers, handwash and so on, and sell online to clients, and, along these lines, keeping up their bank credit accounts sound.

Conclusion

The role of SHG cannot be forgotten, they have put their life into risks and worked for saving lives of other people of the society. Their dedication, their workload and their determination have proved themselves as real heroes working at the ground level for the community level. They have created tremendous social capital which can be utilized to plan successful response to the pandemic..SHGs can showcase their items through Amazon, Flipkart, and so forth. This way they can generate more income to reimburse their bank advances on schedule. Above all, SHG individuals can be granted web-based training in regard of money related/advanced proficiency etc.

Insurance and health benefits should be given to the SHGs workers who are working day and night for the society. SHGs have consistently prevailing because of the adaptability in their activities: This adaptability ought to likewise be the standard in organizations. With the correct help, self-improvement gatherings can have positive effect, when their ladies driven, network based methodology is especially required. Government and development organisations should act to fortify this reliable model. Women in India, and around the globe, have never required it more. They are the change agents and COVID-19 warriors who are selfless and doing their duty like a soldier in the times of serious public health pandemic.

References

African Development Bank Group. (2014). Women's resilience: Integrating gender in the response to Ebola.

Busari, S., & Salaudeen, A. (2020, March 31). 'We don't work, we don't eat.' Informal workers face stark choices as Africa's largest megacity shuts down

Choudhary, A. S. (2015). Economic Empowerment of Rural Women Entrepreneurs in Rajasthan through Self-help Group: A Case of SAKHI. Advances in Economics and Business Management, 2(3), 287-292.

Sudarshan, R. M. (2011). India's National Rural Employment Guarantee Act: Women's Participation and Impacts in Himachal Pradesh, Kerala and Rajasthan.

Ministry of Statistics and Programme Implementation I. Millennium Development Goals: India Country Report 2015. Social Statistics Division, Central Statistics Offfice, Ministry of Statistics and Programme Implementation; 2015.

Ministry of Statistics and Programme Implementation I. Millennium Development Goals: India Country Report 2015. Social Statistics Division, Central Statistics Offfice, Ministry of Statistics and Programme Implementation; 2015.

Government of India. SRS Statistical Report 2011: Office of the Registrar General & Census Commissioner, India, Ministry of Home Affairs, Government of India; 2011

Bihar Rural Livelihoods Promotion Society. JEEViKA, An inititative of Government of Bihar for Poverty Alleviation Patna, Bihar: Bihar Rural Livelihoods Promotion Society; 2009–2010

Vanishri R. Hundekar-An empirical study on "Financial Inclusion through Self Help Groups Bank Linkage Programme – An Economic Catalyst to Transform Rural India"

Ramesh, Jairam. "Self-Help Groups Revolution: What Next?" Economic and Political Weekly 42, no. 36 (2007): 3621-624. Accessed May 13, 2020.

Chapter - 6

Role of Pachayats amidst COVID-19: Study of Sonitpur District of Assam

— Mr. Mohan Pathak

Introduction

Decentralization of power is of utmost importance for every democratic nation to empower people and encourage them to participate in democratic process. Panchayat system of India is an example of democratic decentralization which is directly linked with grassroots people which provides power to the people to actively participate in the democratic activities of the country. Panchayat is one of the oldest democratic and grassroots level self-governing institution of India, whose main objective is to work for the welfare of the rural people. It is also a major administrative tool for socio-economic change of rural area (Sharma & Kalita, 2018. p. 11). The system of Panchayati Raj is also known as local rural government or self-government. It is called self-government because it offers equal opportunities to local elected bodies to solve their local problems or issues by them. According to Mahatma Gandhi, Panchayati Raj is a basic political institution of participatory democracy (Garg, 2019).

Though, Panchayati Raj system in India has existed since Vedic period in different forms, it didn't get constitutional status till 1992. Due to lack of funds, irregular elections, ignorance of the people, insufficient representation, ignorance of political leaders and lack of power, Panchayati Raj institutions of India have not been able to acquire constitutional status. However, on 24 April 1993, it finally got the status of constitutional body under the Constitution's Seventy-third Amendment Act, 1992 and now it is clearly enlisted in the article 243 to 243O of part XI of the constitution. Presently three-tier Panchayati Raj system is prevailing in India; however some States have adopted two-tier Panchayati Raj system.

Today it has been observed that the importance of Panchayati Raj institutions (PRIs) is gradually increasing as it is playing a key role in socio-economic development of people at the grassroots level. There are around 2.5 lakh Gram Panchayts (GPs) in the country who are actively contributing in providing basic services to the local rural people for their socio-economic development (Panda, April 24, 2020).The construction and maintenance of village roads, construction of drains, cleaning of streets, construction of public latrines, constructing buildings of primary education, supply of water for rural people etc are some of the major works that have been done by Panchayats for socio-economic development of rural area.

Apart from socio-economic development, Panchayats also play a pivotal role in political development of grassroots level people. Since it is a grassroots level democratic institution, people can directly participate in the democratic process of the country through this institution. It ensures the political participation and representation of the less privileged group of the society because all eligible voters can directly participate in the elections of PRIs. Moreover, PRIs is also playing an active role as an effective agent of political socialization in rural areas. It has been seen that the rural people are gradually becoming much more aware about political happenings in different parts of the country. Alongside they are also participating in decision making process of Panchayats through which they acquire lots of information about the political process. Because of the reservation policy, the participation of women is also gradually increasing. Women in different parts of the country have been actively participating in different institution of Panchayats despite having lots of social as well as economic challenges.

Moreover, PRIs of India have also been seen quite active during the time of emergency in the Country. This institution plays a pivotal role in management of any crisis in both pre and post crisis period. At the time of any disasters like Earthquake, flood and Cyclone, the PRIs are the most suitable institution to spread awareness and preparedness among the people as well as make the people to be involved in community works. Panchayats also have an active role to play during disaster, because the role of Panchayats in managing disaster comes under major function of Panchayats (Monadal et al 2018). It has been observed that, the Panchayats of West Bengal and Assam always plays effective role in managing disaster in various ways such as providing relief funds, foods, spreading awareness etc.

More recently, after outbreak of COVID-19 pandemic PRIs across the country came to the forefront and played proactive role in country's fight against this pandemic. To mitigate the impact of COVID-19, the Government of India have introduced several measures and PRIs have taken centre stage to effectively implement these measures. In the midst of COVID-19, it is seen that the PRIs of various States actively performed their functions like arranging of quarantine centres, providing relief funds to poor people, distribution of sanitizers, conducting awareness campaigns and sanitization etc. The States like Kerala and Odisha are able to overcome from this pandemic just because of the active role of Panchayats. These states took the help of their PRIs to fight against pandemic and implemented all preventive measures. Presently, around 16 states of the country have given more importance to Panchayats in their fight against COVID-19 pandemic and implement the pandemic strategy (Mahapatra, 24 April 2020). On 24 April 2020, on the occasion of National Panchayati Raj Day, Prime Minister Narendra Modi appreciated the proactive role of Panchayats in fighting against the pandemic. Therefore, this study is undertaken to discuss about the role of Panchayats in the midst of COVID-19 pandemic in Assam with special reference to Sonitpur district of Assam.

Objectives and Methodology of the Study

The major objectives of the study are to discuss the role of Panchayats in the midst of COVID-19 pandemic in Assam and to provide some suggestions to improve the role of Panchayats to tackle COVID-19 crisis.

The present study is both empirical and analytical in nature. The information was collected from both primary as well as secondary sources. The primary data have been obtained through personal interview. Secondary data was collected from Internet, Book, Journals, Government reports and Newspapers etc. As the study was conducted in GPs of Sonitpur district of Assam, hence 5 GPs out of 82 have been selected through simple random sampling. The interview was conducted with officials of this 5 GPs with the help of interview schedule which comprises both open-ended as well as closed ended questions. The collected data were analyzed into percentage and position to achieve the objectives of the study.

The present study was carried out in Sonitpur district of Assam which was created in 1983 after split from Darang. It is spread over an area 5324 sq. km on north bank of Brahmaputra River. It is the second largest district of Assam in terms of area and third largest district in term of population. As per the report of census 2011, the total population of the district is 19,25,975. This district is bounded by Arunachal Pradesh on the north, Biswanath district on the east, Nagaon district on the south and Darang district on the west. The majority of the population of the district is rural and dependent on agriculture. The district has 7 Anchalik Panchayats and 82 GPs GPs which have been playing a very active role in the socio-economic development of the district. The demography of the Sonitpur district is not homogenous in nature as different communities or religious people live in this district such as, Assamese, Muslim, Gorkha, Adivasi, Bengali, Bodo, Mishing etc.

PRIs in Assam and their Role in COVID-19

On 24 April 1993, the 73rdconstitutional amendment Act came in force and it empowered the State legislatures to form Panchayati Raj institutions and also endowed them with necessary power and functions. Accordingly, the State legislature of Assam also passed the 'Assam Panchayat Act, 1994' in 1994 and it finally got the assent of the Governor on 5th May 1994. (Nayak, 2013. p. 1). Currently, three-tier Panchayati Raj system exists in Assam-Gaon Panchayat at village level, Anchalik Panchayat at block level and Zilla Parishad at district level. Presently, these all three level PRIs are actively performing their duties for socio-economic as well as political uplifment of the rural people of Assam.

Along with socio-economic development of the rural people, the PRIs of Assam also play an important role during the time of crisis in the State such as flood, cyclone, famine, earthquake and epidemics etc. Since people of Assam are closely connected with Panchayats so the government of the State always prefer to take the help of PRIs to involve people in all possible preventive as well as protective activities so that the impacts of crisis are reduced and also people are able to protect their lives. It is found that the PRIs are the important institution of disaster management programme of Assam and it works under the District Disaster Management Authority (DDMA). The PRIs perform a proactive role in rescuing and providing relief and before and during natural disaster. They convene meeting to ensure timely warning, organize awareness campaigns, facilitate relief camps, shift people to safe zone, manage medical facilities to the victims, sanitization of affected areas, provide potable drinking water to the people, indentify NGOs and form task forces to provide assistance during disaster etc. after disaster or any crisis in the State.

Dynamic role of PRIs of Assam has been noticed when the COVID-19 pandemic started affecting peoples on socio-economic as well as political arena of Assam like other parts of the country. The role of PRIs became crucial when the Government declared total shutdown and lakhs people of

Assam who were working in neighbouring States started returning to their native places. The Government of Assam provided adequate facilities to those migrant workers and is also taking all measures to prevent the spread of coronavirus in accordance with the guidelines issued by central Government. The PRIs of Assam extended full support to the Government and worked as a core medium of implementation of preventive measures taken by the Government. As learnt from the officials of PRIs, major responsibilities assigned by the Government of Assam to the PRIs are follows-

- Conduct awareness campaigns on COVID-19 pandemic and preventive measures.
- Provide free foods to the poor and destitute and those being kept at the quarantine.
- Deliver financial assistance to migrated workers under PM care fund scheme.
- Sanitize all public places such as shops, markets, medicals, quarantine centres etc.
- Distribution of Masks and Sanitizers.
- Distribution of financial assistance to those poor people who don't have ration card.
- Supervision of quarantine centres which comes under their respective jurisdiction.
- Formation of different level committees to handle the different cases pertaining to COVID-19 pandemic.
- Distribution of financial assistance to the local people providing active contribution to handle the COVID-19 pandemic situation at local level such as Village Defence Force (VDP).

Role of Panchayats of Lohitpur District amidst COVID-19 Pandemic

As already mentioned in the above discussion that the Sonitpur is the third largest district of Assam in terms of population and second largest district in term of area. Since it is one of the populous district of Assam it was also highly affected by COVID-19 pandemic like other districts of the State. The first corona positive case has been reported in the district on 17 May, 2020 and after that the numbers of cases have been increasing rapidly (Tezpur Buzz, 17 May 2020). As per the report of district Administration of Sonitpur district as on 13 August, a total of 2351 corona positive cases has been reported across the district where 1727 have recovered and

3 died. Even though the corona positive cases seem to very high in this district than other district of Assam, however the fatality rate is still not so scary.

There are 82 GPs GPs in Sonitpur district, which has been actively working for the development of the rural people of the district. Like the Panchayats of other district of Assam, the GPs of this district is also performing a decisive role after the outbreak of COVID-19 pandemic. Like the PRIs of other district of Assam, the Panchayats of Sonitpur district also extending their full support and contribution to the Government in the battle against corona virus. It has been seen that the GPs of the district are organizing several awareness programmes in their respective jurisdictions and they are also distributing relief funds, free foods, masks and taking other several preventive measures. Moreover, GPs of this district is also assisting to the central Government in distributing financial assistance which was provided to migrant workers of the States under PM cares fund. Some major functions has been done by GPs of Sonitpur district which are discussed below:

1. Awareness Campaigns

Awareness campaign is the most effective tool to mitigate the impact of any disaster. After the Cvid-19 outbreak, it has been observed that a lot of Government as well as non-government organizations started to organize awareness campaigns so that people can be aware about the causes, effects of the disease and prevention measures. In order to make people aware about preparedness and preventive measures of COVID-19 disease, the GPs of Sonitpur district also organized several awareness campaigns in their respective jurisdiction. To know the role of GPs of Sonitpur district in spreading awareness of COVID-19 disease, five GPs were selected through random sampling method and it has been found from the study

Table 1: Total No. of Awareness Campaigns Organized

Sl. No.	*Name of The Gram Panchayat*	*Number of Awareness Campaign*
1.	DakhinMurhadol G.P.	10
2.	PachhimMurhadol G.P.	10
3.	Uttar Chilabandha	10
4.	Uttar Murhadol	14
5.	Pub Barbhagia G.P.	10
	Total	54

Source: Field Study.

that all five GPs GPs had organized awareness campaigns in each ward of their respective jurisdictions. Through these campaigns, the GPs educated people about many ways to mitigate the impact of this deadly Coronavirus such as maintaining social distance, frequently washing hands, wearing masks etc. The data pertaining to the awareness campaigns organized by GPs of Sonitpur district are mentioned in table-1.

2. *Sanitization*

Sanitization is seen as a strong measure to fight against the COVID-19 disease. After outbreak of COVID-19, the importance of sanitization was highly recognised. It has been observed that the health department of different countries across the globe frequently requested people to sanitized hands, work places, public places and also high contact surfaces etc. to prevent the spread of coronavirus. The Government of Assam also initiated sanitization programme throughout the state and assigned the duty of sanitizing GPs also. The GPs of Sonitpur district also actively participated in implementation of sanitization programme. To investigate the role of GPs of Sonitpur district in implementation of sanitization programme total five GPs were visited and it has found that each GPs provided utmost contribution to implement sanitization programme. They strictly followed the guideline of the Government and sanitized several places such as market, medical sub centers, quarantine centers and banks. The table-2 clearly shows that each GP done sanitization programme in 10 to 17 places and in total 67 places has been sanitized by them.

Table 2: Total No. of Places Sanitized

Sl. No.	*Name of Gram Panchayat*	*Number of Total Places that Sanitized*
1.	DakhinMurhadol G.P.	17
2.	PachhimMurhadol G.P.	14
3.	Uttar Chilabandha	15
4.	Uttar Murhadol	10
5.	Pub Barbhagia G.P.	11
	Total	67

Source: Field Study.

3. *Distribution of Free Ration*

Distribution of free ration to victims of disaster or any epidemics is the prime function of Panchayats across the country. In Assam too, the Panchayats are always seen proactive in providing ration and other necessities during the time of any crisis. It has been found from the study that after outbreak of COVID-19 pandemic the GPs of Sonitpur district have played a pivotal role in distribution of free ration to the poor victims of the people. GPs carried free ration (Daal, Rice, oil, Salt, green vegetables etc.) to the doorstep of every poor families . The study also showed that each GPs distributed free foods to around 3000 to 4000 families of their respective jurisdiction. The table-3 clearly shows the numbers of the families who have received free ration from each of studied five GPs . Moreover, it is seen from the table that these five GPs provided free foods to total 15,100 families.

Table 3: No. of Families Provided Rations

Sl. No.	*Name of Gram Panchayat*	*Number of Families that Benefited*
1.	DakhinMurhadol G.P.	2900
2.	PachhimMurhadol G.P.	2500
3.	Uttar Chilabandha	3000
4.	Uttar Murhadol	3700
5.	Pub Barbhagia G.P.	3000
	Total	15,100

Source: Field Study.

4. Distribution of PM Cares Fund to Migrant workers

The GPs of Sonitpur district made a good contribution in distributing financial assistance to migrated workers under PM Cares Funds. It has been found from the study that the GPs of the district assisted the sub-division offices of their concern area to verify the migrated workers and provides them the relief funds. The officials of some GPs reported that they directly visited to the house of some migrant workers and provided them funds. The table-4 shows the total number of migrant workers who benefited from PM Cares fund distributed by five GPs of Sonitpur district. The table-4 reveals that total 2,154 migrant workers benefited.

Table 4: Distribution of PM care Funds to Migrated workers

Sl. No.	*Name of Gram Panchayat*	*Number of Benefited Workers*
1.	DakhinMurhadol G.P.	492
2.	PachhimMurhadol G.P.	400
3.	Uttar Chilabandha	480
4.	Uttar Murhadol	337
5.	Pub Barbhagia G.P.	445
	Total	2,154

Source: Field Study.

5. Financial Assistance to Village Defence Police

It has been found from study that the GPs of study area also played an active role in distribution of financial assistance to the village defence police who played a vital role in recognition of migrant workers, spreading awareness among the people and taking care of home quarantined people etc. As per the information provided by the officials of five-GPs of Sonitpur district, they provided Rs. 2000 financial assistance to each VDP personnel of their respective jurisdiction from the contingency fund of 14 Finance Commission grants. The Table-5 shows the number of VDP personnel of five GPs of Sonitpur district who benefitted from this scheme.

Table 5: Distribution of Financial Assistance to Village Defense Police

Sl. No.	*Name of Gram Panchayat*	*Number of Total Benefited VDP Personal*
1.	Dakhin Murhadol G.P.	9
2.	Pachhim Murhadol G.P.	9
3.	Uttar Chilabandha	8
4.	Uttar Murhadol	6
5.	Pub Barbhagia G.P.	9
	Total	41

Source: Field Study.

6. Formation of Disaster Management Committees:

The GPs of Sonitpur district also formed different level committees to minimize the impact of COVID-19 in rural area. It has been found a that two level committee- GP level and ward level were formed to deal with the pandemic in GPs. Each GPs formed ward level committees at their respective wards and supervised their functions. The ward member of each ward automatically becomes the member of ward level disaster management committee. The table-6 provided an overview of different level committees formed by five GPs.

Table-6: Panchayats Level Disaster Management Committees

Sl. No.	*Name of Gram Panchayat*	*Total Number of Committees*
1.	DakhinMurhadol G.P.	10
2.	PachhimMurhadol G.P.	10
3.	Uttar Chilabandha	10
4.	Uttar Murhadol	11
5.	Pub Barbhagia G.P.	11
	Total	55

Source: Field Study.

Suggestions

The study shows that the Panchayats of Assam has done several activities to mitigate the effects of COVID-19 pandemic on rural community. However, there are some barriers which do not allow the PRIs to work independently. Therefore some suggestions to improve the role of GPs during the time of crisis are as follows.

1. A permanent disaster management committee should be formed at the GP level consisting of all ward members of the GP.
2. The GP level disaster management committees should train all the skills to be dealt with in times of crisis.
3. The Panchayats should be empowered and encouraged to work actively during the time of crisis by creating a separate disaster management fund.
4. The Government should direct PRIs to organize awareness campaigns on preventive and preparedness skills of disaster in their respective jurisdiction twice in a year.
5. The Government should also direct the PRIs to conduct campaigns about sanitization and its importance.

Conclusion

Looking into the above discussion and facts, it is quite clear that Panchayats of Assam has been playing a very crucial role in preventing and containing the spread of corona virus and in mitigating its adverse effects. Perhaps, due to the notable contribution of Panchayats, the deadly virus has not been able to affect people living in the rural areas of Assam much. Coronavirus has posed a serious threat to the entire structure of the society which is now on the verge of collapse due to loss of huge economic asset. Social normalcy, which is the need of the hour, can be restored only with the active involvement, cooperation and coordination between several agencies and institutions of the government. So, it is highly imperative that efforts be made towards strengthening the power and capacities of the PRIs so that they act as catalyst during the current situations of socio-economic and political instability. So far PRIs have been able to play its role with utmost effectiveness and dedication in mitigating the ongoing COVID-19 crisis and in establishing a sense of confidence in people, and to further enable it to perform its duties in a proactive manner in the moment of any difficulty and crisis, it is necessary to bring internal reforms with an aim to make it more powerful and highly important institution of democracy.

References

Sharma, J. K., & Kalita, D. (2018). *GramyaIsthaniyaPrakhakhon (Assamese)*, Arun Prakashan.

Garg, B. (2019). Village first: Community empowerment on health & development based on Gandhian approach – An experience of working in few villages of Wardha district Maharashtra. *IndianJournalofMedicalResearch*, *149*(7), 63. https://doi.org/10.4103/0971-5916.251659.

Dey, S. K. (1962). *Panchayat-I-raj: A synthesis*. Asia Publishing House.

Panda, P. M. (2020, April 24). *Panchayats as instruments of social and economic progress*. @businessline. https://www.thehindubusinessline.com/opinion/panchayats-as-instruments-of-social-and-economic-progress/article31421460.ece

Mondal, D., Chowdhury, S., &Basu, D. (2018). Role of panchayat (Local self-government) in managing disaster in terms of reconstruction, crop protection, livestock management and health and sanitation measures. *Natural Hazards*, *94*(1), 371-383. https://doi.org/10.1007/s11069-018-3393-x

Mahapatra, R. (2020, April 24). *Panchayati Raj day: Pandemic and the panchayats*. Down To Earth | Latest news, opinion, analysis on environment & science issues | India, South Asia. https://www.downtoearth.org.in/blog/governance/panchayati-raj-day-pandemic-and-the-panchayats-70674

Nayak, P. (2013, December 6). *(PDF)Panchayati Raj in Assam*. ResearchGate. https://www.researchgate.net/publication/250426946

Desk, E. (2020, May 17). First Positive case of COVID-19 that registered in Sonitpur, hails from Balijuri. *tezpur buzz*. http://tezpurbuzz.com/news/first-positive-case-of-COVID-19-that-registered-in-sonitpur-hails-from-balijuri/

Chapter - 7

Role of Panchayats in Managing COVID-19 in Rural Areas

— Ms. Chitra Chandra

Introduction

According to the World Health Organisation, Corona Virus disease (COVID-19) is an infectious disease caused by a newly discovered Corona Virus which can spread from person through small droplets from the nose or mouth which are spread when a person with COVID-19 coughs or exhales.

In the early days of inception, approximately 70 percent of the Indian population residing in the villages, a big source of comfort was that the impact of the Corona Virus disease would be lesser in number than in other countries which has more people living in the urban areas. The rural areas are less densely populated than the urban areas and also has considerably less mobility. Owing to these two factors, it was thought that the spread of the disease would be low. That analysis, however, didn't take into consideration the migrants who desperately wanted to go back to their home in villages. Some walked hundreds of kilometres with families, without food and water while others crammed borders. When the Government finally allowed them to leave and arranged for special trains to take them home, the trains and stations became crowded with the migrants all in desperate urge to go back home any way. Hence with large numbers of migrants already home, or in quarantine centres near their villages and a return path clear for the rest of them, Rural India started growing as hotspot with the disease spreading fast in record time.

COVID-19 is a national challenge which calls for cooperative federalism and this is to be seen as a three-front exercise. Because it is a national issue, it is absolutely essential that the macro picture on policy guidelines be laid down by the Union Government, but with a clear understanding that any large general national policy to influence the outcome will have to require not only the cooperation and whole hearted participation of the State Governments but also the local governments which is PRIs in case of rural areas.

In our Constitution, the inevitability of the Local Government is given constitutional sanction. But apart from establishing a uniform structure of Panchayati Raj in the country as a whole and ensuring reservation for the SC/ST/BC and women which is written in the Constitution, the Constitution mostly has recommendatory suggestions to make including the 11th and 12th Schedules which illustratively set up what is the ambit of work of the Local Self Government units. These are to be translated into statutory powers through State legislation.

So there has to be conformity legislation to bring constitutional provision into legislative effect and all the State Government have done it without exception. So, Schedule 11 and 12 to the extent that they are illustrative in the Constitution have become obligatory and statutory under State law, which by and large have included many other duties and responsibilities for the Panchayati Raj Institutions. In this regard, many State Governments have successfully made the local units of Self Governments active partners in the fight against the pandemic.

Given the seriousness due to the outbreak of COVID-19 pandemic, the Government of India imposed, on 24 March, 2020 a three-week national lockdown (later extended) by invoking provisions of National Disaster Management Act, 2005 (DM Act). The union and state governments were empowered to frame rules and issue executive orders in managing the pandemic situation. The Rural Local Governments, i.e the Panchayati Raj Institutions, which are the basic units of local administration and acts as intermediary between the higher level of administration and the local people, played a key role in containing the spread of the Corona Virus, limiting the numbers from how gigantic it could be to what it is now. Ironically, these key institutions have not found their rightful place in the DM Act. A passing reference is made to 'local authorities' under section 41 of the DM Act. As per the section, these 'local authorities' including panchayats, municipalities and cantonment boards are mandated to carry out "relief, rehabilitation and reconstruction activities" only under the "directions of the District Authority". The DM Act stipulates, under section 25, the constitution of 'District Disaster Management Authority' under the stewardship of district collector/magistrate who is assisted by the Chairperson of the district council in the capacity of co-chairperson of the district authority (Alok, 2020).

Panchayats and Their Fight Against COVID-19

In this tough time, when the current COVID-19 scenario is possibly going to change and reshape a lot of things in the near future, the Panchayats are playing pivotal role in not only fighting the pandemic from the front but also in promoting the economic resurgence. The Gram Panchayats, the smallest unit of the three tier PRIs, being nearer to the people, they are trusted by the communities, and the villagers are dependent on these institutions not only for their basic essential services but also for the livelihood at a large extent.

In this extreme disastrous situation, when the number of COVID-19 cases continues to rise exponentially across the country, the Gram Panchayats have ensured that the response against the crisis includes consultation with the stakeholders and participatory decision making at the lower level. The importance of participatory governance and public discussion in times of crisis has also been emphasised by Prof. Amartya Sen, who says "tackling a social calamity is not like fighting a war which works best when a leader can use top-down power to order everyone to do what the leader wants-with no need for consultation. In contrast, what is needed for dealing with a social calamity is participatory governance and alert public discussion."

Across India, the Panchayats have been prepared and mobilised for grass root action against COVID-19 and they are working closely with the State and District Administration, local health volunteers, ASHA workers, and primary health centres. Any disaster management is highly hierarchical centralised process. But the local government would have to play a very important role because whatever be the broad policy framework, ultimately the action takes place at the local level particularly the relief work and rehabilitation work.

During the pandemic situation, where movement was restricted everywhere so as the keep the infection under control, a large number of migrant workers entered rural India, bringing with them not only the joy of reunion with their families, but also the danger of this disease spreading into those parts of India which were otherwise free of it by then, and the only place that these migrant workers could go and settle is their villages, towns or municipalities. And therefore, while this was to be welcomed, it was necessary to understand that there was a need of the effective delivery of all kinds of assistance to these migrant workers which could only be effectively done by the Gram Panchayats. These institutions of local self-government very effectively worked for the resettlement of the expatriate workers without endangering the local population. Starting from identification, observing and testing these people, to managing the inbound migrants in transit, disinfecting public places, roads & drains, ensuring social security benefits, the local authority had played important roles. To prevent the spread of the virus, the Gram Panchayats have set up local quarantine centres, providing food, drinking water, medicine and counselling to the quarantined people in strong collaboration with the SHG women.

The Gram Panchayats, along with the SHGs, local volunteers and other community-based organisations, undertook huge awareness generation drives on the symptoms and preventive measures of COVID-19. They carried out continuous awareness generation activities among the people through miking, wall writing, social media platform and also using the local media. In addition to that, in many Gram Panchayats house to house visits by the Heads of the Gram Panchayats and other Gram Panchayat Members, ASHA workers, ANMs, Anganwadi workers, community midwifes constantly engaged with the community in spreading the health and sanitation messages, the message that there is no need to panic but need to keep safe and secure by applying social distancing and by taking other precautions was also emphasised strongly. Many Gram Panchayats asked the villagers to remain at home and not to venture out for anything and the significance of social distancing was highlighted at every point of time and also ensured 100 percent enforcement of usage of face masks by all whenever they had to step out of their home. In addition to the Central Helpline, States and many Districts had also developed a COVID-19 Helpline specifically and the details of those helplines were disseminated to every household by many Gram Panchayats. Few Gram Panchayats even provided the contact numbers of all their key functionaries to every home of the village so that the local people need not come out of their home at all for their daily needs and they were insisted to contact any of the key functionaries from the area even for buying food or vegetables or medicine or for any other purpose.

In some States, the Gram Panchayats have utilised the 14th Finance Commission funds for procuring supplies or supporting Self-Help Groups (SHGs) for stitching masks. The SHGs were encouraged to prepare good quality masks at very low cost. This gave tremendous opportunities to the SHG members to acquire the skill of preparing high quality masks at reasonable prices for making them available to the community and also generate income for their groups.

Local solutions cannot happen without decentralisation and giving Gram Panchayats the flexibility to act as per the felt need of the people.

At the moment, Gram Panchayats seem to be tied up under multiplicity of orders and instruction from different departments and higher level of the Governments. In many states, the Head of the Panchayats have been given powers equivalent to the District Collectors to implement quarantine, and utilising those powers many of them have gone to the extent of imposing total lockdown in the Gram Panchayat areas.

Next is the distribution of food grains to the poor and the needy under the Public Distribution System. The Gram Panchayats, in many states, took it as a priority to identify those families not possessing the National Food Security Card among the local population and continuous efforts were being made by the Gram Panchayats to provide ration and cash amount to all the families. Increasing the beneficiaries covered under the Public Distribution System as well as enhancing supplies of essentials such as oil, spices, pulses etc have already been treated as the need of the hour and the Gram Panchayats have put in their 100 percent effort in ensuring this. In many States, Panchayats along with the Self-Help Group members are running community kitchens and providing cooked food to the needy. Gram Panchayats have also shown humane efforts of not only feeding the human beings during this tough time but also the animals in the locality. In many States, the Gram Panchayats are using their Own Source Revenues for purchasing essential supplies, personal protective equipment, hand sanitizers, masks and gloves for the foot soldiers like ASHA workers and voluntary health workers. Many states have given special powers to the Gram Panchayats in regards to enhancing the limit of expenditure from the Gram Panchayat funds for purchasing medicines and foods for the local people and other essential things related to fighting this pandemic situation. Many Gram Panchayats have been successful in mobilising voluntary services and donation to help the poor families in distress owing to poverty, loss of job etc and many were able to collect a lot of donation from the salaried class, upper middle class families, shopkeepers, big farmers and philanthropists in terms of food items like rice, atta, dal, mustard oil, salt, soap and other household items in large quantity and they were distributed among all the needy families in the locality by the Gram Panchayat members dedicatedly. There was continuous provision of assisting welfare programmes by the government, and the Gram Panchayats ensured that in addition to the extra work owing to the management of Covid- 19, the ongoing programmes by the Central and State Government did not go to a full stop.

Next major highlight is an effective coordination with the community-based organisations, various non-profit organisations, political parties, institutions and other key individuals. Continuous efforts were made by these Rural local Self Governments to encourage the community-based organisations to support the Gram Panchayats in identifying the needy persons and delivery of goods and services to the population. Voluntary involvement and active participation of various organisations at this time of distress is definitely noteworthy.

Under the Indian Constitution, the 11th schedule clearly says public health, including primary health centres, dispensaries, hospitals they are all the responsibilities of the Panchayati Raj Institutions. The local Self Governments in normal times also play a very important role in the functioning of the health medical institutions in Rural India. So, it is very obvious that in this health emergency time these rural local self-governments are going to play very important roles. It is very important that how during this lockdown period the Gram Panchayats have been instrumental in ensuring delivery of services like the public health services, the nutrition services. Since the Anganwadi centres were closed during this period, the children were given take home rations and the mid-day meal scheme kept floating in such manner. The Anganwadi workers delivered the rations to the family's doorstep so that the children and the pregnant mothers get at least one meal a day.

In coming days there are few opportunities which we must think of. The COVID-19 pandemic also opens up a big scope of repositioning our Gram Panchayats in public health management system. As is the case of hand wash with soap- actually not many people in rural areas even have the infrastructure of washing hand not to speak of using soap. It has been found that during this pandemic situation this incident of washing the hands with soap has increased nearly double fold, and this improving practice of hand washing with soap can not only prevent COVID-19 but it can also take care of many illnesses which are communicated from hand to mouth.

The Panchayats in our Country have so far been scheme oriented. But if evolution of Panchayats is to take place then they have to behave as a local government independent of the schemes. They should be such empowered that out of their own fund they can immediately jump into the situation and think what can be done in any such emergency situation. So, the local self- governments can really see it as an opportunity to rethink what are the public health activities that can be guided, piloted and steered by the Gram Panchayats, because many preventive activities are not medical interventions, these are social interventions, these are behavioural change interventions requiring lot of monitoring, lot of guidance, lot of enabling and empowering of the community level which gives the opportunity now and even after the COVID-19 pandemic is over and can reduce the contagious diseases transmitted from hand to mouth and thus can control the incidence of such pandemics.

How Can Panchayats Prepare to Leverage Opportunities

None of us actually know how long this COVID-19 pandemic is going to continue. We are not certain whether the problem will be solved in few months or it will take few years. Till the time there is a vaccine or medicine for COVID-19 becomes available, prevention is the only option. In prevention of COVID-19, there are two things which are mentioned- first is social distancing and the second is hand washing and maintaining good sanitation. But for both we need the cooperation of the local people. For social distancing people has to be told what is social distancing and how that can be achieved. Panchayats are the best institutions who can continue generating this awareness among the rural community. Second is water supply and sanitation. Now, though under the Constitution responsibility of providing water supply and sanitation facilities is assigned to the Panchayats, many a times these are carried out by line departments of the State Government. The Panchayats can legitimately do that in the future. This is further supported with the fact that the 15th Finance Commission has given 50 percent of their fund as tied grants for water and sanitation related activities.

During the period of lockdown and even now in the slow unlocking phase, what really happened is that when the people in the urban areas wanted to get fruits, vegetables and milk, farmers in the rural areas were thinking how to sell their harvest. There comes the role of the Panchayats. The Panchayats can help strengthen local livelihood opportunities and also market local production by identifying the sources of demand and supply and by facilitating the market linkage process between the suppliers and the consumers. If decentralised community-based approach to managing disasters in general and COVID-19 in particular has to become a reality, then local self-governments have to play the role of social mobilisation centres, rather than just benefit distribution centres.

Panchayat level Disaster Mitigation plan is to be prepared where all the functionaries of the Panchayats and the officials involved with the Panchayats is to be trained. We have National Disaster Mitigation Plan; we have State Disaster Mitigation Plan but we do not have a Panchayat Disaster Mitigation Plan. We also have a National Disaster Response Force; we have State Disaster Response Force, but there is no Community Disaster Response Force. So, Community Disaster Response Force is the need of the hour now and they have to remain with the rural local self-governments actually.

Next comes how the Panchayats can be really empowered to tackle the economic problem which has emerged with people coming back as migrant workers. The Panchayats can identify who are the people who have migrated back to the village, what are their skills and how they can be employed, should it be in the wage employment programmes or in the self-employment programmes. The Gram Panchayats can also identify the raw materials available in that area and ensure that with the raw materials available and the skills which are now become available can they start a micro small or medium enterprise in the village. Today in the Skill Development Programmes at the local level we have trained the rural folks, the rural youngsters in all the skills to be utilised in the cities and as a result the whole range of primary skills which are necessary to make our rural life better, rural life more interesting, more exciting are missing in these skilling programmes. Of course, there are primary skills, but that has never got priority in the skilling delivery system. So, Primary Skill Building Programmes will become the major agenda along with the migrant database of the Panchayats. This migrant database is a must now that should be prepared by the Panchayats for resettling the rural economy and the lives of the migrant workers. This will add to making self-reliant villages and lead to self-reliant India.

MGNREGS is one of the major flagship livelihood generation programmes in India. Strengthening this programme will help the most vulnerable and needy group to generate a livelihood, and also effectively working on it with a proper plan can lead to creation of new opportunities as well. The rural local self-governments can play a vital key role in context-based planning and better implementation of MGNREGS in such situation.

It is very necessary now to develop our Gram Panchayat Development Plan in such effective way through participatory approaches so that all the migrants can be accommodated in the development process in their respective areas and it will definitely boost the livelihood generation process.

Again, now would be the time to create an effective peer to peer learning network where the rural local self- governments can learn from the experiences of others within the same State and across States. Panchayats can be one of the effective institutions to help people at the grass-root level and Panchayats can always support in manifold ways and as an administrative entity it would be easy for the Gram Panchayats to take the voice of the local people to the top level of administration which may impact good governance and policies.

Conclusion

Actually, it is not the Country that is fighting with this pandemic, but it is the people who are fighting with this pandemic. Every major crisis, such as the Coronavirus (COVID-19) pandemic, brings opportunities to rethink our systems and make them more resilient to future shocks. This is also true for rural regions. One of the primary lessons of COVID-19 is the primacy of the local. Local governance, local leaders, local communities and local organisations, when empowered, respond to any disaster rapidly and effectively. This is because of three distinct strengths and the significant advantage they bring (Kapur & Panicker, 2020). First, is the practical consideration of local level knowledge. Due to their proximity, panchayats are usually the first point of contact for most citizens and thus best placed to know about mobility, as well as, social security needs. Community-level engagement and dissemination of information become an easier task than deploying resources from the state level. Second, administratively, while their functions vary, panchayat members are the nodal point across most social welfare programmes and have the power of direct reach in their hands. They can play a vital role in ensuring that welfare services get delivered on the ground and no person is left behind from accessing relief packages for want of documentation or lack of knowledge. Finally, from the citizen perspective, the panchayat represents the quintessential community. Appropriate local representation in planning and coordination efforts provides an opportunity for true state-local and citizen action, particularly in times of crisis. The current COVID-19 crisis has once again re-emphasised the importance of decentralised governance. They need information and guidance, but they should also have resources, capacities and systems in place to act with confidence, without waiting for instructions from above.

The Panchayats which are really the people's institution has been the unsung warriors who have not only worked for limiting the spread, but also gone extra miles to ensure that the essential services are not disrupted, especially for the vulnerable.

References

Kapur Avani and Panicker Aishwarya. (2020). This National Panchayati Raj Day, Local Governance is More Important Than Ever Before. The Wire, April 24.

Retrieved from https://thewire.in/government/national-panchayat-day-COVID-19-management-local-governance

Shylendra, HS. (2020). How is COVID-19 playing out in rural India? The Hindu Businessline, May 25. Retrived from https://www.thehindubusinessline.com/opinion/how-is-COVID-19-playing-out-in-rural-india/article31671013.ece

Shoo, Niranjan. (2020). Panchayats and pandemic. ORF, April 25. Retrieved from https://www.orfonline.org/expert-speak/panchayats-pandemic-65185/

Tandon, Rajesh. (2020). Trust & empower panchayats to respond to COVID-19. Times of India, 27 April. Retrieved from https://timesofindia.indiatimes.com/blogs/voices/trust-empower-panchayats-to-respond-to-COVID-19/

Mahapatra, Richard. (2020). Panchayati Raj Day: Pandemic and the panchayats. Down To Earth, April, 24. Retrieved from https://www.downtoearth.org.in/blog/governance/panchayati-raj-day-pandemic-and-the-panchayats-70674

Mitra, Shouvik. (2020). The implications of COVID-19 for rural India. IDR, March 25. Retrieved from https://idronline.org/the-implications-of-COVID-19-for-rural-india/

Vijayanand, S.M (2020). Kerala's management of COVID-19: Key learnings. Retrieved from https://www.ideasforindia.in/topics/governance/kerala-s-management-of-COVID-19-key-learnings.html

Raghunandan TR. (2020). Responding to COVID-19 at the grassroots. The Hindu, May 1. Retrieved from https://www.thehindu.com/opinion/op-ed/responding-to-COVID-19-at-the-grassroots/article31552359.ece

Jha, Vikas. (2020). How can gram panchayats respond to COVID-19? IDR April, 28. Retrieved from https://idronline.org/how-can-gram-panchayats-respond-to-COVID-19/

Alok, V N (2020), Local governments must have a key role to fight COVID-19. Financial Express, June 1. Retrieved from https://www.financialexpress.com/lifestyle/health/local-governments-must-have-a-key-role-to-fight-COVID-19/1977869/

16 June 2020, Policy implications of Coronavirus crisis for rural development, http://www.oecd.org/coronavirus/policy-responses/policy-implications-of-coronavirus-crisis-for-rural-development-6b9d189a/

https://www.who.int/emergencies/diseases/novel-coronavirus-2019/question-and-answers-hub/q-a-detail/q-a-coronaviruses

https://www.ruralhealthinfo.org/topics/COVID-19

KILA, May 16, 2020, National Webinar on- The COVID-19 Pandemic and Local Governments.

Chapter - 8

Impact of COVID-19 on Rural Wage Employment: Analysis of MGNREGA

— Dr. Rajesh Kumar Sinha

COVID-19 in Rural India

As per World health organization, COVID-19/is/a disease/caused by a new strain of coronavirus. 'CO' stands for corona, 'VI' for virus, and 'D' for disease. Formerly, this disease was referred to as '2019 novel coronavirus' or '2019-nCoV' (WHO, 2020). The disease spreads primarily through contact with an infected person when they cough or sneeze and virus gets released with tiny droplets. It also spreads when a person touches a surface or an object that has the virus on it, then touches her/his eyes, nose, or mouth. Therefore, it is recommended worldwide that one can protect oneself by washing hands frequently, avoiding touching face, and avoiding close contact (1 meter or 3 feet) with people who are unwell. The most common symptoms of COVID-19 are fever, tiredness, and dry cough. Some patients may have aches and pains, nasal congestion, runny nose, sore throat or diarrhea. These symptoms are usually mild and begin gradually. The World Health Organisation (WHO) reported that there is no currently available vaccine for COVID-19 and that several research institutes and laboratories are at various stages of developing vaccine. First case of COVID-19 was found in India on 30th January 2020 and since then it has been increasing continuously. On 28th August, 2020, total cumulative 34,63,972 cases of COVID-19 has been reported in the country. However, recovery rate is also quite high and mortality rate is decreasing marginally. Although initially, COVID-19 cases remained concentrated to urban areas, of late constant surge in the number of cases reported from rural areas has been witnessed. The virus has spread to about 711 of 739 districts, including 100 of the country's poorest rural areas. Several districts in nine major states — Bihar, Madhya Pradesh, Telangana, Jharkhand, Uttar Pradesh, Maharashtra, West

Bengal, Odisha and Gujarat — all of which have sizable rural populations, are highly vulnerable to new infections, according to a Lancet study (Pradhan, 2020). On August 10, 2020, rural and semi-urban centres accounted for 47% of fresh infections, or almost double their share as compared to a month ago. Fresh infections in semi-urban regions rose faster than those in rural areas, from 13.3% of the country's total infection a month ago to 27.3% on August 10. The urban share of new infections during this period fell from 75% to 53%. In terms of new deaths, rural areas are growing faster than any other areas. While the share of urban areas in fresh daily deaths fell to 69.7% on August 10, from 84.2% a month ago, that for semi-urban areas rose to 18.5% from 10.1%. The share of rural areas, however, more than doubled to 11.8% from 5.7% earlier. In terms of total infections – not just fresh infections – rural and semi-urban regions now account for over a one-third of total cases. They accounted for a 20% share a month back. By the month-end, rural and semi-urban regions may account for nearly half of total infections (Gera, 2020).

MGNREGA

The Mahatma Gandhi National Rural Employment Guarantee Act, 2005 (MGNREGA) was notified on September 7, 2005 and was launched on 2nd February 2006. The mandate of the Act is to provide at least 100 days of guaranteed wage employment in a financial year to every registered rural household whose adult members volunteer to do unskilled manual work (Ministry of Rural Development, 2008). The Ministry mandates the provision of additional 50 days of wage employment (beyond the stipulated 100 days) to every Scheduled Tribe Household in a forest area, provided that these households have no other private property except for the land rights provided under the FRA Act, 2006. Central Government has decided to provide an additional 50 days of unskilled manual 10 work in a financial year, over and above the 100 days assured to job card holders in such rural areas where drought or any natural calamity (as per Ministry of Home Affairs) has been notified. Every registered household is issued a job card which contains the updated details of work demanded and received, wages paid etc. Goals of the Scheme, inter-alia, are (i) social protection for the most vulnerable people living in rural India by providing employment opportunities (ii) livelihood security for the poor through creation of durable assets, improved water security, soil conservation and higher land productivity and (iii) drought-proofing and flood management in rural India (Ministry of Rural Development, 2016). Wage seekers have (i) right to get work within fifteen days of application or from the date when work is sought in the case of an advance application, whichever is later (ii) right to get 10% extra wage in case of employment provided beyond 5 km of radius (iii) right to get wages paid on a weekly basis or in any case not later than a fortnight after the date on which such work was done (iv) right to get unemployment allowance in case employment is not provided within fifteen days of submitting the application or from the date when work is sought in the case of an advance application, whichever is later. Panchayati Raj Institutions (PRIs) at the GP, Block and District level are principal implementing authorities. Gram Rojgar Sahayak (GP), Programme Officer (Block) and District Programme Coordinator (District) assist PRIs in implementation of MGNREGA. All workers have a right to participate in the Gram Sabha/Ward Sabha and decide the works and the order of priority to be taken up under Mahatma Gandhi NREGA for their Panchayat. The Schedule – I of the Act provide list of permissible works categorised into 4 parts. Based on the various works mentioned in the Schedule, the Management Information System (MIS) has listed 43 categories of works covering 260 types of works 31 permissible under the Programme. Of this, 181 works are related to Natural Resource Management of which 84 are water related works. 164 works are related to agriculture and allied activities. Contractors can not be engaged and machines can not be utilized in carrying out works under MGNREGA. Wage material ratio of 60:40 is prescribed. Workers will paid daily wage notified for agriculture labour in the State (Ministry of Rural Development, 2013).

At present, MGNREGA is being implemented in 692 districts, 6923 blocks and 2,64,585 Gram Panchayats/ Village Councils. In MGNREGA total 13.67 cr. job cards have been issued and out of these 7.61 are active job cards. There are total 26.65 cr. workers registered under MGNREGA and out of these 11.7 cr. are active workers. Among active workers schedule caste workers are 19.1 percent and scheduled tribes workers are 16.3 percent. Progress of MGNREGA in last four financial years is given in table below:

Progress	***FY 2019-2020***	***FY 2018-2019***	***FY 2017-2018***	***FY 2016-2017***
Total Persondays Generated [In Cr]	264.46	267.96	233.74	235.64
SC persondays % as of total persondays	19.72	20.77	21.56	21.32
ST persondays % as of total persondays	18.29	17.42	17.49	17.62
Women Persondays out of Total (%)	54.67	54.59	53.53	56.16
Total Households Worked [In Cr]	5.47	5.27	5.12	5.12
Total Individuals Worked [In Cr]	7.87	7.77	7.59	7.67
Differently abled persons worked	4,55,576	4,61,880	4,72,218	4,71,819
Number of Ongoing Works [In Lakhs]	116	106.84	122.93	97.08
Number of Completed Works [In Lakhs]	71.32	90.22	62.63	65.46
Total Financial Expenditure [In Cr]	67,701.82	69,618.59	63,649.48	58,062.92
Wages Paid [In Cr]	48,553.2	47,172.55	43,128.49	40,750.72

Source: http://mnregaweb4.nic.in/netnrega/all_lvl_details_dashboard_new.aspx

MGNREGA's Role in Reducing Rural Distress Due to COVID-19

In response to increasing incidence of COVID-19 cases, the Government of India announced a complete lock down on from 23rd March to 14th April 2020 which was extended three times with some progressive relaxations, first up to 3rd May, second up to 17th May and third up to 31st May 2020. Impact of COVID-19 was felt on rural wage employment opportunities. During the lockdown, worried of uncertain future and also lack of adequate support, migrant labour from urban areas moved back to their villages. At the same time due to lack of agricultural inputs and also off take of agricultural produces, demand for labour in agricultural operations in these areas declined. All other economic and business activities in rural areas also came to stand still due to restrictions on movements of vehicles making daily wagers unemployed for at least two month period from the announcement of first nation-wide lockdown. Initially, MGNREGA activities also stopped, but Government realised that it had to be started so as to provide wage employment to unemployed villagers and reverse migrants in distress. The agriculture sector operations came to a standstill, especially harvesting of perishables and other cereal crops, and preparation of land for the coming season. Though the summer months are peak for the MGNREGA works, the labour required for harvesting operations is also high in these months especially, the areas where vegetables/fruits are cultivated, and paddy and wheat harvest is commencing. Since the lockdown prevented the movement of labour from one area to another, a severe shortage of hands for harvesting these crops was felt in certain areas. In terms of number, MGNREGA can reach out to 39 percent of the rural households in business as usual scenario. It can go up to a maximum of 69 percent of rural households if all rural household having job card demand work, that might happen with minimal probability. The migrant labours who returned to the villages demanded jobs under MGREGA. An increase in labour supply has been witnessed due to reverse migration. In response, Government of India took two important measures, first increase in the daily wage from Rs.182 to Rs.202 and second, additional allocation of Rs.40,000 crore to MGNREGA making the total allocation Rs. 100,000 crore for the FY 2020-21. In a subjective estimate, a minimum of 15 crores people may have demanded to work under MGNREGA during the stressful first quarter of the financial year 2020-21.

Changes Needed in MGNREGA in the Wake of COVID-19

In a scenario like above when there is high demand for job and also scarcity of labour for agricultural operations, inclusion of harvesting and sowing operations under permissible MGNREGA works, irrespective of the size of the farmland, to avert food crisis may be an option. Though the kind of stressful period witnessed in the month of March, April and May is over, COVID-19 and its effect is going to stay for at least a year from now. Hence certain changes in the design and processes of MGNREGA are needed to respond to the situation.

Any adult member from registered household whose name is included in the job card can demand work under MGNREGA irrespective of their age group, education health and marital status. Most of the workers are non-disabled adult members and belong to the age group of 18 to 60 years. Also women participation is high in many states. Around 12 percent of the workers belong to the old age group, and 2 percent goes to the category of disabled and people facing debilitating health issues. The old age and people with health issues fall into a high-risk group as fatality rate from COVID-19 is found to be high among these groups. As a precaution, it may be wise to find an alternative way of supporting old age and people and other people with serious co-morbidity by providing light works, even during harvesting or any other agriculture operations with maintaining physical distancing. For example, such persons may be allowed to work in the maintenance of horticulture plantations, watering, weeding, sorting, watch and ward etc. Soil and manure filling in the grow bag for raising sapling and kitchen garden etc. during the current disaster. During the harvesting, food for the labours can be provided through community kitchens with contribution from farmers.

For entire of this financial year 2020-21, MGNREGA need to be implemented following social distancing. The work should be seen as a combination of tasks and each task consist of different activities. Some activities are independent, while others are not. The adult workers can focus on works that have independent tasks because it is possible to keep workers more than one meter if tasks are independent. All types of plantation works, including horticulture, can be promoted, as these works and related tasks are independently performed. Additional such works like harvesting or raising kitchen garden for short term vegetables may be identified and added into the approved list of works.

In absence of livelihood opportunities in urban areas and due to lack of adequate support, huge numbers of rural families have moved back to their villages during the lockdown and are without work and income. Many of such migrant workers may not be part of the list of card holders and hence they may have problems of becoming part of MGNREGA works.

Hence, a special system has to be put in place for enabling all such families to get benefitted by MGNREGA works.

As indicated earlier, MGNREGA may be linked to agriculture during the next one year. An ongoing pan India study conducted at NIRDPR (one-decade assessment of MGNREGS) based on 7604 sample households from 25 states shows that 38 percent of these wage seekers are landless and remaining families belong to marginal and small landholders. As far as the income of these workers is concerned, a rural household earns Rs. 8,666 per year. It is a contribution of around 9.5 percent of the total income of a rural household. The income varies across States within a range of 7 to 17 percent of the total household income. In addition, marginal and small farmers benefit significantly from MGNREGA in terms of category B assets created in their farms. There is a strong interconnect between MGNREGA and agriculture. Today both labours and farming community are under distress. Therefore, linking MGNREGS activities with harvesting and other agricultural operations for a limited period may create a win-win situation for both workers and farmers.

Presently, a single muster roll consists of 20 to 25 members depending upon the number of available workers. Viability of completing work within a week is also a concern while preparing the muster roll. Joining of different muster roll is also practised in large projects like desilting of a bigger tank or river rejuvenation etc. As a result, few category 'A' works were implemented with a maximum of 415 people in many worksites which can be avoided in the present context. These large projects can be replaced by small projects that can be implemented within a week with a maximum of 9 people in one muster roll. Monitoring of distance keeping, maintaining hygiene will be easy if the number of people is less in muster roll. Special muster roll can be introduced for old age and unhealthy people for maintenance work in plantations.

Implementing agencies are supposed to provide facilities of safe drinking water, shade for children and periods of rest, first aid box with adequate material for emergency treatment for minor injuries etc. at MGNREGA worksites. However, adequate first aid, shades are not provided in many of these sites. There is a need to improve the worksite facilities for maintaining personal hygiene. In addition to above facilities, provisions should also be enabled for supplying face mask, hand washing facility or hand sanitizers at the work sites.

Timely job and payment of wages are crucial to enhance the income security of the poor people through MGNREGA. Different communication channels like internet, phone, or oral communication must be encouraged for demanding the work. Delay in payment of wages within 15 days must be avoided. Selecting work with less material and skilled labour may help to maintain sufficient fund under labour component for the next few months.

To make use of the opportunity of producing face masks/hand sanitizers that are required for preventing spread of COVID-19, in the community, their production can be promoted with quick training, using ICT tools through these workers. In every village, at least 10-15 families, who otherwise would be looking for work, can be enabled to produce face masks/ hand sanitizers, that the Gram Panchayat can procure to distribute to all the people in the village/Gram Panchayat. The work period can be accounted under MGNREGA to give those families wages and also at the same time.

And last but not the least, portability of MGNREGA job card may also be considered. Because in a situation like the lockdown and restriction of movement coupled with lack of employment, willing migrants can claim their rights under MGNREGA in the nearest rural district if such portability is enabled with the help of MIS of MGNREGA.

Conclusion

MGNREGA has the potential to provide solution of lack of wage employment in rural areas and also scarcity of labour for critical agricultural operations like harvesting, sowing, watering etc. if these activities are included under list of permissible MGNREGA works. Realising this potential and responding to the increased demand for jobs under MGNREGA, Government of India has provided additional Rs. 40,000 crore for implementation of MGNREGA. This will not only provide much needed income support to rural poor and reverse migrants, but also boost rural economy by increasing demands. By ensuring social distancing and personal hygiene facilities at worksites, ensuring regular and timely payment of wages, tasks in isolation for old and people with co-morbidities, skilling of MGNREGA workers in making masks, hand santizers, hand wash etc., MGNREGA can further serve as an important vehicle to contain spread of COVID-19 in rural areas and provide necessary income support to rural poor and reverse migrants who are in distress.

References

WHO. (2020a). Naming the Coronavirus Disease (COVID-19) and the Virus that Causes it. Retrieved from https://www.who.int/emergencies/diseases/novel-coronavirus-2019/technical-guidance/naming-the-coronavirus-disease-(covid-2019)-and-the-virus-that-causes-it on 20.08.2020.

Ministry of Rural Development. (2008). National Rural Employment Guranatee Act, 2005 (NREGA) Operational Guidelines 2013 3rd Edition. Government of India. New Delhi.

Ministry of Rural Development. (2013). Mahatma Gandhi National Rural Employment Guranatee Act, 2005 (Mahatma Gandhi NREGA) Operational Guidelines 2013 4th Edition. Government of India. New Delhi.

Ministry of Rural Development. (2016). Mahatma Gandhi National Rural Employment Guarantee Act, 2005: The Journey of A Decade. Government of India, New Delhi.

[Inputs from Centre for Wage Employment, NIRD&PR and from Prof. Jyotish Satyapalan is duly acknowledged by the author.]

Chapter - 9

Impact of COVID-19 on Rural Economy of India

— Ms. Anindita Mukherjee

Introduction

COVID-19 was first declared as a public health emergency and later a pandemic by the World Health Organization (WHO). More than 213 countries/territories have been affected so far by the deadly virus. There was National emergency and lockdown in most of the countries. In the span of a few months, COVID-19 pandemic has devastated health system and the economies of countries including economy of some developed countries. According to Ministry of Health and Family Welfare, Government of India, at the end of July more than 20 lakh people have been affected, more than 50 thousand people are getting affected per day and around 50 thousand people have lost their lives in just 4 months due to this disease.

The world was taken by surprise completely by the rapid spread of COVID-19 virus worldwide from its original epicenter in Wuhan, China. This pandemic found both the Central Government and the State Governments in varying degrees of unpreparedness. But Governments reacted reasonably quickly to combat the situation, as saving lives was the priority of the Government. The Epidemic Diseases (Amendment) Ordinance was promulgated on 22nd April, 2020 amending the provisions of the Epidemic Diseases Act, 1897 and Central Government announced certain measures in 4 phases of lockdown started from March 25, as lockdown can slowdown the spread of the infection as well as provide time to health systems to deal with the disease at multiple levels. However, the effect of lockdown has come at an economic cost to all sections of the society throughout the globe.

The Linkage between Public Health and Economic Health

There is close connection between health sector and the economy. The illness and the loss of life due to COVID-19 will put excessive burden on healthcare system and it has both immediate and continuing effects on the economy. Immediately it would be on wages and income which would increase large-scale poverty and destitution. In the long run health care would also impact human resource formation and there would be loss in human capital. In the long run it would affect the health, education and infrastructure sector also.

Issues and Challenges in the Rural Economy

After the Economic liberalization (initiated in 1991), due to higher growth India became the fifth (5th) largest economy in the world in terms of Purchasing Power Parity (PPP), but it also created rural-urban disparity and agriculture remained the prime source of livelihood for most of the population. Still now majority of the people in this country live in abject poverty and even now hunger persists. It ranked 102 out of 117 countries in the Global Hunger Index 2019.

Due to lockdown broadly three kinds of rural activities have been affected: agriculture and allied activities, local non-farm sectors and rural-urban migration. Slowdown of economic activities in urban areas had an effect on the income of rural people as most of the rural migrant labourers are engaged in different urban activities such as construction work, electrical work, painter, driver, cooks of different hotels and restaurants, sales person of different showrooms, security guard etc. who are the support hands to every sector of the economy. As lockdown was announced suddenly, to arrest the spread of virus, millions of labourers became jobless, foodless and even shelter less. Though it was declared a national disaster and Government had made it obligatory for the employers to pay the wages as per National Disaster Management Act, but many enterprises did not comply especially financially weak enterprises.

Challenges in Agricultural Sector

Agricultural sector is being seen as the oasis in the desert of economic crisis as it engages almost 60 percent of rural workforce. But this sector also suffered a significant loss in respect of production, harvesting, distribution and exports. The beginning of the COVID-19 pandemic has coincided with the peak harvesting season of Rabi crop and the time, when the farm harvests reach the market place (mandis) for guaranteed procurement by government agencies. It was a threat to several hectares of agricultural land in the country which affects the farmers as well as the agricultural labourers. As there were movement restrictions, border closure and social distancing, to contain the disease, some problems emerged immediately with the lockdown which can be described as follows:

(i) **Fertilizer shortage**: Farmers are facing shortage of agricultural inputs like fertilizers and pesticides which will create problem in the long run as the interruption in supply chain disturbance continues.

(ii) **Labour unavailability**: Due to reverse migration there was shortage in agricultural labourers which resulted in severe increase in labour cost for harvesting. Some farmers were compelled to allow their crops to rot in the fields itself which affects the availability of food.

(iii) **On food production**: Most of the agricultural produce is perishable in nature. Due to stoppage of transportation, farmers were forced to hold their unsold produce which had reduced the food quality. Also due to joblessness of large section people due to lockdown, there is reduction in the overall demand for food which in turn has a negative impact on the farmers.

(iv) **Cash flow constraint**: The loss of the farmers created huge problem in repaying their crop loans which means that they have to borrow from private money lenders for the next harvesting season.

Challenges due to Reverse Migration

Most of the Indian population is engaged in informal sector, which have no job contract, no social security and no benefit of paid leave. Though there is Social Security Act for unorganized sector's workers (2008) but only 5-6% got enrolled for social security. In this current scenario, the return of the migrants to their home states, because of massive lay-offs, creates big challenges on the rural economy in the prevalent situation. This can be explained as follows:

Population size will change along with features of that place. The returnees have come with empty hands, putting pressure on the economy of that village.

(i) Majority of the returnees were marginal farmers in the past. Their return creates immense pressure on agricultural sector which was already in a crisis over the past two decades because of low productivity, scarcity of water, increase in input costs etc.

(ii) Increase in rural unemployment and poverty will have adverse impact on livelihood that will lead to chronic food insecurity among the rural poor.

(iii) There is a fear of contamination from the virus as there is a population pressure which will have adverse effect on health system of the rural areas and there might be chances of community spread.

Other Issues and Challenges

(i) Problem of selling: Though the production of few essential items continued, they faced difficulties because of low consumer demand, fragile and breaking transport system, close down of mandis and rural haats which created acute problem for the small farm holders to sell their produce.

(ii) Problem of distribution: When lockdown was announced people could not go to their place of work and so production stopped. As production of goods and services is concentrated in only few pockets and distributed throughout the globe, the supply chain of goods and services was hampered with an adverse effect on the rural economy.

(iii) Exogenous factor: The USA-China trade war was an exogenous factor affecting our economy as they are the world's two largest economy.

(iv) Effect on Women: Women are suffering a lot due to this economic crisis. The fast mechanization in agricultural sector has reduced their participation in the labour market. The income of Self-Help Groups also decreased due to dearth in aggregate demand in the market and was overburdened with care work. The income losses are creating a vicious cycle of low demand, low savings, low investment and low income.

(v) Effect on Children and their Education: Severe economic stress, due to joblessness, put the children and in particular the girl child at a risk of becoming child labour and beggar and victims of exploitation, trafficking and gender-based violence. Children are also at risk of psychological distress at time of crisis. The number of child marriages and child trafficking in rural areas of several states has strikingly become higher due to the lockdown as the family has no or a little amount of money to spend for their girl child. As the schools are closed and the education system is fully running through online mode, it cannot give access to all children and several children dropped out from this system, especially children of penniless migrants.

Unlocking and Recovery

After the three-phase lockdown, started from 25th March, 2020, Government had decided to unlock the country in phased manner outside the containment zone from June 1, 2020 to bring economic activities back in track which was totally in a distress for the long-time complete lockdown. Due to health-economic trade-off, economic deterioration was visible clearly and there was a situation that lives could be lost by deprivation of job and food, instead of virus which is normally unacceptable. Because as manufacturing and distribution chains of different sectors were frozen for long time period, there were severe disturbances in the supply chain of labour and so, the number of unemployed people increased in huge number, mainly in the densely populated states which creates huge burden on the economy. So, the nation has been shifting attention to focus on the economic activities where COVID-19 and economic re-opening will run parallelly.

It is the belief of many economists that after reaching the all-time low level of this year, the economy will go ahead towards recovery in the next financial year. But some economists like Pronab Sen, former Chief Statistician of India, observed that the economy will contract not only for this year but also in 2021-22 and India may face full-scale depression for

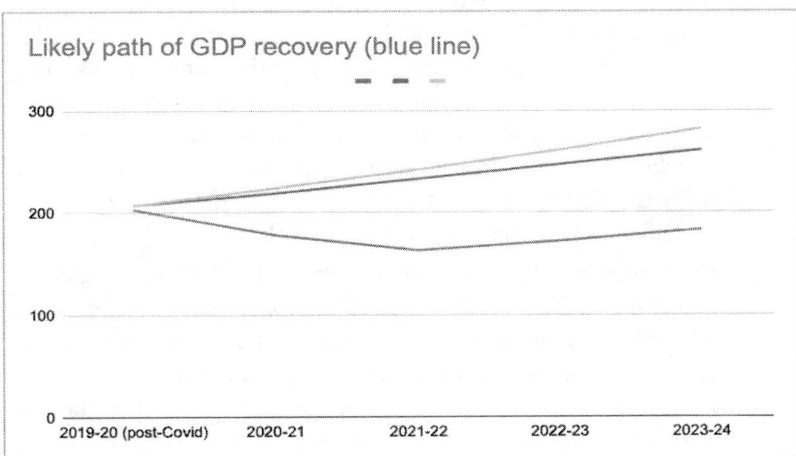

the first time in history of India after Independence. So, it can be said that given the fragility of the economy, moving through the COVID-19 crisis as well as low fiscal impetus, India may end up with an elongated 'U-shape' retrieval as shown in the graph below. (Mishra Udit, The Indian Express, New Delhi, June 8, 2020)

Lessons from the Crisis and Policy Measures

The world is experiencing such type of pandemic for the first time to combat this kind of invisible enemy. It is very important to learn lessons from the pandemic situation and for the roles of Central/State/Local governments, centralization versus decentralization of power by the governments, the transparency and effective communication to all stake holders etc. The two principles of development, both Cash Transfer as well as Public Distribution System (PDS) are complementary to each other and not the alternative and government should apply both in this crisis period as our main objective is to save the lives of the disadvantaged (Maitreesh Ghatak and Amitava Gupta, Ananda Bazar Patrika, July 17, 2020).

Government of India has taken several measures, some immediately after lockdown and some later in the lockdown phases to provide relief to the distressed people which are mentioned below:

(i) The immediate measure was the announcement of Rs. 1.70 lakh crore as Prime Minister's Garib Kalyan Yojana (PMGKY) Package on March 26, 2020 just after the lockdown started. It was imagined to guarantee food security by providing 5 kg wheat/rice per person, per month and one kg pulses free per household for three months (now it has been extended to November 2020), cash transfers of Rs. 500 per month for the next three months in Jan Dhan accounts of 20 crore women, ex-gratia payment of Rs. 1000 to senior citizens and widow and increase in wage rate of MGNREGS from Rs. 182 to Rs. 202. For benefit of 8.7 crores of farmers Rs. 2000 crores were given to farmers under Prime Minister Kisan Yojana. Collateral free loan was doubled to 20 lakhs from 10 lakhs to support the SHGs.

(ii) On 12th May, 2020, our Hon'ble Prime Minister announced an economic package of Rs. 20 lakh crore for revival of the economy which was moving towards deceleration and to make our country self-dependent. It included the earlier package of Rs.1.7 lakh crore under PMGKY. This package involves agricultural infrastructural development of Rs. 1 lakh crore, Rs 30,000 crore as an emergency working capital for farmers through NABARD and Rs. 10,000 crores for micro food enterprises to build cluster-based approach. All these funds were planned to make strong the post-harvest infrastructure, dairy infrastructure, investment in cattle feed, honey farmers, herbal and medicinal plants etc.

(iii) To meet the huge demand in the agricultural labour market, due to reverse migration, the government allocated an additional Rs. 40,000 crores to MGNREGS for the FY 2020-21.

(iv) The economic package also included Rs. 6000 crores to augment forestry and to benefit the tribal population.

(v) On 3rd June, three ordinances came out in agricultural field which are (a) Essential Commodities (Amendment) ordinance, 2020, (b) Farming Produce Trade and Commerce (Promotion and Facilitation) Ordinance, 2020, and (c) The Farmers (Empowerment and Protection) Agreement on Price Assurance and farm Services Ordinance, 2020 which are being viewed to transform Indian agricultural sector.

(vi) In the sphere of Micro, Small and Medium Enterprises (MSMEs), collateral free loans value of Rs. 3 lakh crores were assigned in the form of Guaranteed Emergency Credit Line (GECL) facility so that the MSME sector can expand.

The measures are being criticized as most of them are based on long-term reforms instead of providing liquid cash to the underprivileged to enhance the effective demand of the economy. The recent ordinances of curtailment of different provisions of labour laws by several State governments like Uttar Pradesh, Madhya Pradesh, Punjab and Uttarakhand for capturing investments are being criticized for a labour-unfriendly approach which may cause deterioration in the working condition of the workers and exploit them more. The revenue-starved government has taken a long time to raise MGNREGS spending in mid-May, 2020.

Opportunities and Policy Measures Needed

Crisis gives us opportunities too. Social entrepreneur and Nobel laureate Muhammad Yunus is of the opinion that this pandemic has created a chance for the entire world to rethink the concept of the economy and while visualizing plans and policies we should acknowledge the informal sector which largely comprises the poorer and rural sections of the society. Economy begins with the formal sector and the informal sector had never been recognized as the poor were never the primary concern of the policy-makers. (The Telegraph, August 1, 2020)

India observed reverse migration for the first time since independence. So, there are more development opportunities for redefining investment priorities. More investments in the rural sectors especially agro-based industries can generate new jobs for the displaced labourers, who are in grave humanitarian crisis. It can strengthen rural sector's economy and share in GDP as well.

Skills of the reverse migrants can be gainfully utilized locally which they have acquired so far. The rural economy can become self-reliant by doing this and also growth process will be decentralized. Some infrastructures are to be needed for this purpose. State governments have to think to build industrial hubs, setting up MSMEs for feasible projects which can generate employment opportunities that can boost up the economic growth through multiplier effect.

The aggregate consumption demand has been worsened and the consumption pattern changed also due to the lockdown induced disruption in the supply chain of goods and services and joblessness of several people which was already in the rough path for the last few years. So, augmenting the consumption demand at the earliest is the need for the hour since consumption expenditure accounts for almost 60 (sixty) percent of India's GDP. Government should provide cash transfer to the bottom 60 percent of people to help in reviving the economy as advocated by Nobel laureate Abhijit Binayak Banerjee. He also opined that increasing the spending power of people may be a better option than a package specially targeted for MSMEs. Spending money will create a stimulus effect on consumption as propensity to consume of the poor people is always high. (The Print, 16th July, 2020)

Nurkse's theory (1953) of 'Unlimited Supply of Labour' in less developed countries says that if the surplus labor in the economy can be utilized with the productive labour together, the potential source of savings will be increased. Harris and Todaro added that the growth of the informal sectors in the urban industrial sector is because of this rural-urban migration. So, the time is to use the reverse migrants as potential source of savings which will increase investment in multiplier effect in their home states. If this can be done it might be a critical support for the economy. Vibrant demography is our source of energy for self-sufficient India.

Immediate and Short-term Policy Measures to Revive the Tottering Economy

(i) India needs a large stimulus package to boost up the economy from financial depression.

(ii) There is a necessity to remove the restrictions of 100 days of employment, participation of one person per household etc. Timely wage payment is also very crucial in time of distress. Migrants should be enabled to join this programme by a simple process.

(iii) Instead of RBI announced five-month loan holiday on all term loans to help the borrowers facing temporary financial difficulties, it may be cancelled even for that quarter and may be taken care of by the government.

(iv) Investment friendly policies would be required for boosting up private investments. There is a scope of generating different development models and an opportunity for redefining investment priorities. In the rural sectors multiple scopes are there such as allied products of agriculture, food processing, traditional Indian handicrafts etc. India needs to increase its exports too.

(v) Education will play an important role to lift up our healthcare and also to build a productive economy. This is the right time for India to boost its e-education and e-healthcare systems also in the rural areas so that the poor and distressed people can take the benefit of it through the Panchayati Raj system.

A strong determination and several bold reform measures are required to be taken to make the nation self-sufficient so that the effect of such type of pandemic in future can be nullified. We have to explore opportunities from the crisis which can give us lessons about the importance of local level manufacturing and local level supply chain so that during crisis majority of our demands can be met locally and it can also extend the hands beyond the geographical boundary. Within these reforms, agricultural sector reforms are very important where an indestructible supply chain is needed.

Simple and clear laws, capacitated human resources and a powerful financial system are required apart from the rational tax system. These reforms can augment business, bring investment and strengthen our country. The rural economy, through the 3-tier Panchayati Raj system can envision of out-of-box approach in a mission mode to uplift the hemorrhaging economy. The GPDP (Gram Panchayat Development Plan), for the next financial year (2022-2023), should focus on welfare of people and local economic development including agriculture and skill development of local youths specially the women, so that they can move with a dignified livelihood and the local government can move towards Sustainable Development Goals (SDG, 2015-2030).

In India, a legacy of self-reliance already exists. The Nehruvian model of self-sufficiency, balanced between the global and local aspects, acts as a stimulus for India's self-reliance. This model of self-sufficiency had been preceded by another, the Mahatma Gandhi's model, where 'local' was the fulcrum around which the engine of development was revolved. Gandhiji had shown the truest form of 'atmanirbharata' or self-reliance which helped the most vulnerable section of the society where the last man and woman could stand on their feet.

Conclusion

When COVID-19 was declared as a pandemic no one imagined the changes it would bring. Economic activities had come to a standstill, output and production collapsed, leading to significant loss of livelihood which has driven the economy beyond the economic boundaries.

It has been repeatedly said by the experts that a demand stimulus needs to be created and putting money in the hands of people is absolutely essential. But it has to be kept in mind that inflation rate should be controlled in this harrowing situation. Presently, Inflation poses bigger threat and is above 6% as the economic picture remained dismal with both industrial production and service sector activity showing contraction and due to hike in food price. The role of RBI is very important in this respect as there is a growth gloom and the GDP of the country is likely to contract in this fiscal year, the first such instance in over four decades. The Monetary Policy Committee is conscious about reducing the inflation rate. Tax reforms in India are part of broader set of fiscal reforms. So, we should adopt a rational, well-defined and more inclusive tax structure.

At the same time, as the economy is moving through a downward path so, economic activities need to be continued throughout the country in all the sectors. Though we have to keep in mind about the containment of the disease, but lockdown should be invoked only in the containment zones instead of the whole nation or whole state.

Both the Central and State governments have to utilize and enhance the allotment of the MGNREGS programme, the safety net in rural areas, in more expanded and inclusive way so that the returnees can get jobs and do not compel to return back to the cities in this pandemic situation.

Business and industries will have to adapt to the 'new normal' phase by maintaining norms of sanitization and keeping physical distancing. Small business units can shift their production line to the high-demand products applicable to 'new normal' time to achieve greater economic activities.

Once the pandemic is controlled, government should rethink seriously about our development strategy to run the economy in future. While framing the policy, the models of Adam Smith, Karl Marx and Mahatma Gandhi should be explored and be used judiciously. The first model is the non-interfering demand-supply model, where the invisible hands of market will control the aggregate demand and supply. But there is a problem of unequal distribution where the disadvantaged remain outside the market mechanism. So, the focus should be on just distribution to alleviate economic exploitation which was propounded by Karl Marx. In the present situation, the victims of lockdown-the agricultural, construction and migrant labourers, should get the privilege of proper distribution system. Long term planning and policy decisions are required to address the grave problems of distribution. Gandhian model emphasizes on consumption limitation and sharing resources with others, which has a moral and ethical angle. So judicious use and combination of the referred models may provide the appropriate solution for planning and policy formulation.

References

Banerjee Chandrajit, Director General, Confederation of Indian Industry, The New Indian Express 13.06. 2020.

Chowdhury Dhar Praheli, Ananda Bazar Patrika, 17.07.2020.

COVID-19 and its Impact on Agriculture, Civil Daily, 06.06.2020.

Dey Satyagopal, Ananda Bazar Patrika, 17.07.2020.

Ghatak Maitreesh,Gupta Amitava, Ananda Bazar Patrika, 17.07.2020.

Harris, J.R. and M.P. Todaro (1970): Migration, unemployment and development.

Krishnaprasad Suchita, Migration & Economic Growth, YOJANA, June 2020.

Misra Udit | New Delhi | Published: 08.06.2020, The Indian Express.

Nurkse.R, (1953): Problems of Capital Formation in Underdeveloped Countries. Oxford University Press.

Prasad Urvashi,COVID-19: India's Response and the Way Forward, Kurukshetra, June 2020.

Raghuramaraju. A, 'A medical emergency and the need to help the underprivileged: Three options', The Telegraph, 06.04.2020.

Reddy. W. R, Mamgain. P. Rajendra, P,Revival and Reconstruction of Rural Livelihoods amidst COVID-19: Policy Responses, Opportunities and Way Ahead SRSC Policy Paper Series - 1/2020, National Institute of Rural Development and Panchayati Raj.

Yunus: 'Chance to recognize informal sector', The Telegraph, 01.08.2020.

https://indianexpress.com/article/opinion/corona/virus-india-lockdown-economy-amartya-sen-raghuram-rajan-abhijit-banerjee-6364521,

https://debrajray.com/wp-content/uploads/2020/05/RaySubramanian.pdf, https://mpra.ub.uni-muenchen.de/100530/ MPRA Paper No. 100530, posted 20 May 2020 20:39 UTC

https://www.globalhungerindex.org/india.html

https://indianexpress.com/article/explained/explainspeaking-when-will-indias-economy-recover-shape-of-its-recovery

https://indianexpress.com/article/explained/why-indias-gdp-growth-rate-is-being-labelled-an-overestimate-yet-again-6436503/

https://theprint.in/opinion/india-revial of economy-abhijitbanerjee-raghuram rajan-16.07.2020

Chapter - 10

Impact of Covid -19 on Handicraft Clusters in India

— *Ms. Jasmeet Kaur*

Introduction

Handicraft have been perceived to be royal and belonging to patronage, also played an important role in Gandhi's struggle, but now seems to loose relevance due to advent of industrialization (Chamikutty, 2013). Different handicrafts products have relevance in Indian history after the name of the clusters.

An age old phenomena, Clusters are well known in India since centuries. Clusters are concentration of units in a particular area making similar or same products. Clusters face common problems and threats and look forward to similar opportunities.According to the report of Foundation for MSME Clusters (FMC), "2010 Clusters of India",India has more than 6400 clusters amongst which some are famous for their products at domestic and international level.

Clusters can be classified as handloom, industrial and handicraft. This paper specially concentrates on the impact of COVID-19 on handicraft clusters of India.A representation of Socio – economic heritage of our country, as some towns or villages are specially known for their products existing for decades and centuries. A cluster usually covers few villages or a city and its surroundings or few blocks of district (Bhattacharyya, 2013).

Clusters represent rich tapestry of India's past and present rich heritage, but still little is known about them, their contribution, problems, relevant policies and revival initiatives taken by government in last decade.

Table 1: List of Some Famous Handicrafts Clusters

Cluster Name	*State*	*Famous For*
Handloom Cluster of Chanderi	Madhya Pradesh	Traditional Chanderi Sarees
Handicraft Cluster of Moradabad	Uttar Pradesh	Brassware
Hand block Printed Textiles Cluster	Jaipur (Bagru), Rajasthan	Hand Printed Fabrics
Tirupur Cotton Hosiery cluster	Tamil Nadu	Cotton Hosiery
Ludhiana Knitwear cluster	Punjab	Knitwear

Currently, this sector has a stigma of "inferiority" and "backwardness", this is because of the negative aspect of government not focusing on the industry in past. Lack of good policies and programmme for the protection and upliftment of the artisans was required (Chamikutty, 2013).

To enhance productivity related to production of rural cluster of artisan, government initiated MSME, for modernizing the approach and providing substantial effect in livelihood of artists. (Bhattacharyya, 2013)

For upliftment of these clusters, Micro and small Enterprises – cluster development programme (MSE-CDP) is an initiative by government. Earlier to this Cottage and small industry department was taking care of all rural artisans. But now more rural artisans, clusters as well as individuals are trying to opt for this scheme by government to gain benefits (Bhattacharyya, 2013).

Micro enterprise clusters producing products related to handicrafts and handlooms are known as artisan clusters. The main advantage of a cluster is that it makes the availability of skilled labour for that particular craft easy and fast exchange of information in regards to technology related to craft and commerce most efficient. Some issues are resolved taking collective decisions. This helps government also to extend support for people under same umbrella.

Despite different initiatives by government time being, major obstacle is to compete with technological advancements that aid industry that produces cheap and better finished goods. Handicraft is typically perceived as old fashioned, traditional and in compatible to modern taste (Chamikutty, 2013).

Marketing of the handicraft goods also is a major issue prevailing, as competition from conventional products are high. Lack of organized industry and professional behavior adds to a point where a product needs to be availed to specific brands or bigger retailers. It is a time taking process to upgrade artisans livelihood and introduce changes (Bhattacharyya, 2013).

Chamikutty, 2013, states major challenges faced by handicraft artisans for sustaining a livelihood in today's world are -

1. Low productivity by the sector being informal. Outdated method of production. Low education adds to the frame.
2. Low input, Low raw material quality, lack of design inputs, inadequate funding.
3. Less marketing linkage, influence of middle men, broken value chain Negligence by government, lack of interest amongst new generation.

Objectives

1. To understand the condition of the Handicraft clusters of India.
2. To study the impact of covid -19 on Handicraft clusters of India.
3. To find out the initiatives taken by government and different stakeholders.
4. To identify the "New Normal" challenges & opportunitiesfor handicraft clusters of India.

Literature Review

Cluster is well known by the name of product it produces and place they are located in. They face similar opportunities and threats and can be divided in traditional industry cluster, handicraft cluster and handloom cluster.

Different schemes from government helps these handicraft clusters to upgrade, revive and aid assistance like Scheme of Fund for Regeneration of Traditional Industries (SFURTI), Industrial Infrastructure Up gradation Scheme (IIUS), Cluster Development Program, Baba Saheb Ambedkar Hastshilp Vikash Yojana (AHVY), NABARD, etc .

Amongst, all states, Uttar Pradesh tops with 282 handicraft cluster, Orissa has 271 clusters, West Bengal with 245 and Gujarat with 199 clusters. This is a reflection of India's rich heritage.

Chamikutty, 2013, in its report, divides craft sector into five different segments .Frist segment is Organizations which includes Self Help Groups (SHGs), Private Limited Companies, Mutually Aided Co-operatives (MACs). Second division is processing and procuring and raw materials, which is easily available because of usage of locally available material. Third segment is production which is seasonal, as artisans perform agricultural practices during non-seasonal period to earn livelihood. Market being the fourth segment divided as local retail shops or high end exhibitions and expos. Fourth segment being demand which lacks due to competition from contemporary market.

But Covid -19 affected the economy and many different segments of it severely. India is one highly effected country with its handicraft sector facing challenges (McKeever, 2020). This study emphasis on the impact of COVID-19 on Indian handicraft sector (Muro, 2020; Macksoud, 2020).

During usual situations also the handicrafts segment undergo different challenges of survival, but handicraft clusters are on the verge of collapsing, as there are no orders in the month of May and June which is considered a busy time for manufacturing for upcoming season (Bailey, 2020).

Theoretical Framework

After the review of literature, a theoretical framework has been formulated. The frame work is designed considering the prevailing challenges, impact of COVID-19 on handicraft sector, post lockdown challenges and opportunities.

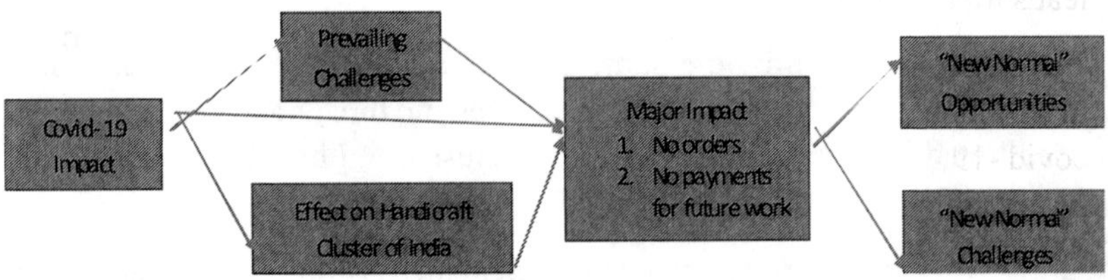

Figure 1: Theoritical Framework

The study uses the above framework for understanidng the impact of COVID-19 on handicraft sector by studying the prevalling challenges, major impact due to COVID-19 pandemic economic and health crisis and later "New Normal" opportunities and threasts .

Methodology

After the topic selection, a framework was developed which was used as a basis for study. The data which is used in the study is secondary in nature. Literature has been searched from previous reviews, newspapers and reports.

For data collection, from February 2020 to July 2020, online media has been searched regularly for knowing updates related to COVID-19 effect on apparel industry. The main complication while data collection was that still not much information is available other than newspaper and online media (Sen, 2020).Few journals have been cited. Newspapers like Hindustan times, Times of India, Mint live etc, have been reviewed. After the data was collected, analysis of information was done.

Impact of COVID-19 on the Handicraft cluster

Handicraft doesn't falls under essential commodities, the difficult situation of people form this sector also doesn't attracts coverage from media in this current pandemic. People from different clusters are dependent on orders from big designers and brands. (Bose 2020).

An article by Indo Asian News Service, 2020, states that Covid-19 pandemic impacted not only specific nation but the whole world and has lasting effects on population health and economy. Sudden disruption in businesses all over the world and in India too, handicraft sector too got effected severally. Traditional and contemporary market of artisans being completely closed face losses. It has affected the basic livelihood of the artisans.

As crises unfolds, no sign of immediate recovery is seen. Adversely effected cash flow, buyers not able to make payments, lack of sales, does leads to a conclusion that the recovery will be slow.

Buyers are not placing orders as orders are received 2-3 months prior to sale time .due to social distancing and strict norms to avoid spread of covid -19, infection, retail events are suspended for next few months which hosted like a main source of sale and income generation for artisans (Indo Asian News Service, 2020).

Another problem seen is change in customer priority due to less purchasing power. Small artisans lack in financial power back up to hold through financial crises for long, thus feeding families are another bog task. Free ration help from government is acting like a help through tough time, but facing difficulties to curb basic medical needs (Indo Asian News Service, 2020). Makeovers, 2020, claims that this pandemic outbreak is not only a global health crisis, but also a major labor market and economic crisis.

One big question that arises is "What is the actual need to the handicraft artisans –to get actual work to earn livelihood or to survive with funding / donation?"

Initiatives taken to support the Handicraft Cluster:

Sally (2020), claims that, as per the current situation of the industry, government has been requested (The Confederation of Indian Textile

Industry (CITI),to announce immediate relief packages to reduce the crisis faced by capital and labour intensive industry.

As the outspread has led to haul at domestic sales, the market for Indian handicraft has impacted a lot (Sally, 2020). As a response and taking responsibility of the workmen's, many different initiatives have been taken by stakeholders and brands.

Few active measure have been taken by government, self-help groups and NGO's working at ground level, to safeguard rural population. These initiatives include continuation of supplying of middle meal and aganwadi meals. Few states like Kerala, government also took initiative to avail food meals at door steps for children and pregnant women. Another initiative includes supplying free ration with the help of public distribution system.

Government also tried to reach rural population through its Jan Dhan Yojana crediting 500 rupees in poor women's bank account. With PM-KISSAN scheme, 2000rupees has been credited to farmers account. Local groups are extending support to ASHA workers and civil society groups, working through this tough time.

But also it is retailors and brands responsibility to take of people working closely with them and for them. Head of Crafts at Tata Trusts, Sharda Gautam, states that while facility of Incubation & Design Centre across clusters in Odisha, Nagaland and Assam are closed, help has been extended in terms of increasing the use of internet and digital payment systems, which in turn helped to fight with loss of orders. These clusters are comfortable with technology and thus know ways to reach out to consumers using platforms like WhatsApp, email and social media. More training has been given through Antaran, which is an online knowledge centre on YouTube .Thus this time is being used by artisans to bring improvements in product catalogue, increase online presence and reorganize inventory.

Artisan-entrepreneur, Imran Kasim from Varanasi, claims that around 200 workers are working with them, but distributing less work and extending extra payments, we are trying to deal with the situation by not reducing the number of weavers. Designer of Brand Mantra, Shalini James, states that they helped many weavers, karigars and tailors were helped to migrate to home towns, in hope to return when things get better (Bose 2020). Few workers who stayed back, helped in making reusable mask for police personnel's of Kerala state, maintaining social distance and high order cleanliness (Bose 2020). Cherai Handloom Weavers Co-operative Society, are paying money for work done from home by weavers who have looms at home. Others who don't have looms will be compensated with some payments (Bose 2020).

Challenges of "New Normal"

There is a state where an economy or society settles after a major crisis. This situation of "new normal "differs from the previous prevailed situation. Thus it is important to understand the challenges and opportunities that relates to new normal. Post COVID-19 lockdown situation has been addressed as situation in "new normal".

After the lockdown, the industry will take a longer time to recover. Mishra, 2020, claims that it may take few months, to get everything back to normal. But it is tough to foreseen the uncertainty of future times. Recovery for strong financial companies are expecting faster recovery.

Following are the challenges of "new normal" that all sectors have to face-

1. Migration of Labor for workplace: Labor force migrated to villages and home town has to return back where factories are situated. But this could cause problem as social distancing may not be maintained.
2. Interrupted supply chain – Due to effect on import and export and effected transportation, supply chain has been interrupted largely.
3. Less investment in handicraft products – As this product segment is not in essential commodities, consumers investing in handicraft product is less. The purchasing power is affected.
4. Cash liquidity – Lack of financial assistance will lead to lack of working capital post covid lockdown also.

Opportunities of "New Normal"

Following are the opportunities that tentative to prevail in "new normal" after the crisis-

1. As the festival time is approaching, this is the time precious to retailers and manufactures. October '20 will be considered as indicator in justifying the real change in consumer segment, in relation to festival sentiments and purchase behavior. This time can be used as an opportunity to revive future business.

2. Putting less emphasis on bulk production or sourcing for the upcoming seasons, as planning for four to six months further should be done in order to first sell what is piled up as inventory.
3. People will be conscious about hygiene, thus safety or consumers and employees should be the first step post lockdown in the new normal. Using designs of products and techniques of manufacturing that leads to a better hygienic and clean product, may lead to more sales.
4. The future sustaining of any business online presence. Online sales are key to future business. As consumer have likely develop a habit of avoiding crowd and ordering online, this may continue as a consumer behavior to prefer online shopping more than offline mode. Thus handicrafts being available online on famous websites selling with other complimentary products seems to be a good opportunity.

Conclusion

Covid -19 pandemic has shaken worldwide economy, future is difficult to predict as time is uncertain. Because of pandemic the whole supply chain got affected, handloom and handicraft clusters from rural India being the most effected from the textile industry. Support from government is limited, with no work, no means to earn livelihood, the situation is vulnerable. With government supplying basic free ration, involvement of multi stakeholder was also important to curb in the economic and health crisis (Sen, 2020).

Since the study was dependent on secondary data, hence primary data from specific handicraft clusters as target group can be collected and studied to understand different aspects.

Quantitative analysis focused on how the sudden pandemic created health and financial crises. Special target groups like women workers can be studied for future study.

Literature lacks on work for the impact of Covid -19 on the rural clusters of handicraft and handloom sectors of textile and apparel industry. Thus this study is one of its first study to specifically focus on the prevailing challenges and opportunities of handicraft clusters and their vulnerable condition during the pandemic time. As this paper studies few examples of initiatives taken by different groups, brands and stake holders for survival of clusters in Rural India, this gives a scope of further study. Impact of initiative by government and multi stake holders to be studied as future study. The study suggest post lockdown opportunities that can be supportive to business organizations and brands to make plans for future adjustments.

References

Anner, M. (2020). Abandoned? The Impact of COVID-19 on Workers and Businesses at the Bottom of Global Garment Supply Chains. Center for Global Workers' Rights Research Report (27 March 2020), https://www. workersrights. org/wp-content/uploads/2020/03/Abandoned-Penn-State-WRC-Report-March-27-2020. pdf (accessed 10 May 2020).

Bailay, R. (2020, June 25). [Web log post]. Retrieved 2020, from https://economictimes.indiatimes.com/industry/cons-products/fashion-/-cosmetics-/-jewellery/indian-fashion-industry-on-the-verge-of-collapse/articleshow/76532111.cms?from=mdr

Bhattacharyya, D. (2014). Cottage industry clusters in India in improving rural livelihood: an overview.

BOSE, S. K. (2020, May 11). What About Weavers? How India's 2nd Largest Employment Sector Is Dealing with COVID-19 [Web log post]. Retrieved 2020, from https://www.thebetterindia.com/225439/designers-weavers-artisans-weaving-hand-loom-industry-north-east-COVID-19-coronavirus-impact-sustainability-india/

Cernansky, R. (2020). As coronavirus spreads, supply chain workers face layoffs. Voguebusiness.Com. Retrieved from https://www.voguebusiness.com/sustainability/coronavirus-causes-closures-and-layoffs-forworkers-bangladesh-india.

Chain, T. V. (2020, August 5). Impact of COVID-19 on Sambalpuri Handloom Society [Web log post]. Retrieved 2020, from https://textilevaluechain.in/2020/08/05/impact-of-COVID-19-on-sambalpuri-handloom-society/

Chamikutty, P. (2013, June 19). Problems facing the Indian artifacts sector [Web log post]. Retrieved from https://yourstory.com/2013/06/crafting-a-livelihood-a-snapshot-of-the-indian-artifacts-sector-2#:~:text=Low%20productivity%20%E2%80%93The%20sector's%20informal,space%2C%20shipping%20and%20packing%20facilities.

Duffin, E. (2020). Impact of The Coronavirus Pandemic on The Global Economy-Statistics & Facts. Statistica Report, April, 3, 2020.

I. (2020, April 19). COVID-19: Weaving threads of hope in the times of Coronavirus [Web log post]. Retrieved from https://www.hindustantimes.com/fashion-and-trends/COVID-19-weaving-threads-of-hope-in-the-times-of-coronavirus/story-0aszQBkpfoUMZcjtwPdi9O.html

I. (2020, April 19). Handloom weavers staring bleak future following COVID-19, lockdown [Web log post]. Retrieved from https://www.onmanorama.com/lifestyle/news/2020/04/19/mpact-COVID-19-on-indian-handloom-sector.html#:~:text=Prime%20hurdles%20that%20COVID%2D19%20has%20caused&text=Retail%20events%20through%20which%20artisans,things%20get%20back%20to%20normal.

Kamruzzaman, M., &Sakib, S. N. (2020). Bangladesh imposes total lockdown over COVID-19. Anadolu Agency.

Khubchandani, S. (2020, March 19). Coronavirus Impact on Indian Crafts and Handlooms [Web log post]. Retrieved 2020, from https://thevoiceoffashion.com/centrestage/business/coronavirus-impact-on-indian-crafts-and-handlooms—3643

McKeever, V. (2020). CORONAVIRUS Nearly 25 million jobs could be lost globally due to the coronavirus, UN labor organization estimates. CNBC.

Mishra, S. B., & Singh, S. R. COVID-19: POST LOCKDOWN CHALLENGES AND OPPORTUNITIES FOR READYMADE GARMENTS SECTOR IN INDORE CITY.

Muro, M., Maxim, R., &Whiton, J. (2020). The places a COVID-19 recession will likely hit hardest. The Avenue.

Sen, S., Antara, N., Sen, S., & Chowdhury, S. (2020). The apparel workers are in the highest vulnerability due to COVID-19: a study on the Bangladesh Apparel Industry. Sen S, Antara N, Sen S, Chowdhury S. The apparel workers are in the highest vulnerability due to COVID-19: a study on the Bangladesh Apparel Industry. Asia Pacific J Multidiscip Res, 8(3).

Sen, S., Antara, N., Sen, S., & Chowdhury, S. (2020). The apparel workers are in the highest vulnerability due to COVID-19: a study on the Bangladesh Apparel Industry. Asia Pacific J Multidiscip Res, 8(3).

Sen, S., Antara, N., Sen, S., & Chowdhury, S. (2020). The Unprecedented Pandemic "COVID-19" Effect on the Apparel Workers by shivering the Apparel Supply Chain. Journal of Textile and Apparel, Technology and Management, 11(3).

Singh, A. (2010). Clusters in India. Foundation for MSME Clusters (FMC). Retrieved August, 3, 2015.

Chapter - 11

Impact of COVID-19 on Rural Self Help Groups (SHGs)

— *Dr. Shafia Wani*

Introduction

From ancient time, human civilisation has been facing a lot of constraints and challenges in its sustainable developmental phase among which poverty seems to be the most disastrous one. India, as a second largest democratic country in the world, is also facing such problem which seems to be one of the vital barriers for inclusive growth as well as to compete with other developed and developing countries in several dimensions. Therefore, special attention is to be assured to eradicate poverty through which livelihood of general populace can be developed and in this context, rural poor should especially be addressed. Respecting this issue and welcoming inclusive growth for socio-economic excluded poor people mainly from rural boundary, different developing and underdeveloped countries time-to-time declared various promotional and developmental programmes. In this context, Deendayal Antyodaya Yojana, National Rural Livelihood Mission (DAY-NRLM), implemented by the Central Government of India has become the World's largest poverty alleviation scheme. Hence, it is very essential to visualise the practical application and acceptance of the welfare prospect of the very Mission in rural vulnerable populace. This effort is materialised successfully with the measurement of the sustainable livelihood promotion as introduced by the said scheme for the marginalised rural poor attached with a socio-economic backward area. Apart from that Self-Help Groups (SHGs) have emerged as an increasingly effective tool of collective empowerment of women. The women's movement that started as a leap of faith some 15 years ago has proved to be an invaluable resource in these difficult times. Over the past two decades India's SHG movement has evolved from small savings and credit groups that sought to empower poor rural women, into one of the world's largest institutional platforms of the poor.

The COVID-19 outbreak has affected all segments of the population and is particularly detrimental to members of those social groups in the most vulnerable situations, continues to affect populations, including people living in poverty situations, older persons, persons with disabilities, youth, and indigenous peoples. Early evidence indicates that that the health and economic impacts of the Coronavirus generated disease are being borne disproportionately by poor people. For example, homeless people, because they may be unable to safely shelter in place, are highly exposed to the danger of the virus. The coronavirus disease (COVID-19), which has been characterized as a pandemic by the World Health Organization (WHO), is attacking societies at their core. As India fights the Coronavirus disease (COVID-19), it requires all stakeholders to take charge and deliver. Several efforts were made by the government, civil society organisations (CSOs), SHGs(women led collectives), panchayati raj institution (PRI) members and the local administration to facilitate this process. These included provision of food and transport, creating shelters, and building awareness in the interior areas.

Among those which are working on the ground, the women-led self-help groups (SHGs) have emerged as effective frontline responders, reaching the last-mile and ensuring an immediate relief and socio-economic protection to the country's most vulnerable. Their reach is staggering: Approximately 67 million women are organised into 6 million SHGs. Operating on the principles of self-help, cohesion and mutual interest, SHGs are voluntary groups of 10-20 women from their neighbourhood, who pool their savings and gain access to credit. As of today, these collectives have saved $1.4 billion, and leveraged another $37 billion from commercial banks. What began as a call to empower poor rural women under the aegis of the Deendayal Antyodaya Yojana-National Rural Livelihoods Mission (DAY-NRLM) has since grown into one of the world's largest institutional platforms for the poor.

Role Played by SHGs Amidst COVID-19

Women at the center of development are playing an important role in these extraordinary times, when we are all united in our fight against the COVID-19 virus, these women's groups are playing a critical role. The sensitivity and responsiveness demonstrated by SHGs amid the COVID-19 crisis at the community level is highly commendable.

With huge numbers of informal workers losing their livelihoods during the lockdown and food supply chains getting disrupted in some areas, SHGs have set up over 10,000 community kitchens across the country to feed stranded workers, the poor, and the vulnerable.

In Kerala, the Kudumbashree network, one of the country's earliest community platforms of women with 4.4 million members and several years of catering experience behind them, were the government's natural choice to run a number of these kitchens. Given the massive nature of the challenge, these groups have dramatically ramped up their efforts and are now running 1,300 kitchens across the state, while also delivering food to those in quarantine and the bedridden. Notable efforts have been made by women of Kudumbashree in Kerala, to help dispel the widespread fake news that causes panic. Through its network of WhatsApp groups with 1,16,396 Women as members, Kudumbasree is trying to propagate only the right information to the community. These platforms are used specifically to disseminate immediate, authentic information and updates on the outbreak and precautionary measures.

In Bihar, women under the JEEVIKA platform (the State Rural Livelihood Mission) are active in identifying and surveying vulnerable households. Using innovative communication methods, SHG members ensure that the risks of COVID-19 and its transmission are easily explained to rural masses. Using the information education and communication material developed by the state mission, the didis, as they are locally called, use the network of 1.4 lakh state-wide SHGs to create awareness about hand-washing, social distancing, sanitation and quarantine. JEEViKA is trying to systematically reach out to a maximum number of households through its 1.4 Lakh SHGs and spread the awareness on topics such as handwash, sanitation, quarantine and isolation and social-distancing. JEEViKA has till date collected mobile numbers more than 1,00,000 of community members and is using the Mobile Vaani platform to release voice messages on COVID-19 and is also addressing the community's queries through the same.

In Uttar Pradesh, with the help of Khadi Gramudyog, SHG members plan to produce masks worth six lakh metres of khadi fabric. In Kheri district, SHGs are working round-the-clock to produce PPE kits for frontline health workers and police personnel. Moreover, SHG women under the Prerna platform use methods such as rangolis, videos and songs to create awareness about hand-washing and social distancing.

In Jharkhand, SHG women use the Aajeevika Farm Fresh mobile app to sell vegetables, ensuring that social distancing guidelines are not flouted. They also use their networks to identify vulnerable households, flagging to the administration the pockets in need of food. They help run a 24-hour helpline by the State Rural Livelihood Mission (SRLM), which provides important information and counselling to the returning migrant. Every Panchayat in the state has a Muhkya Mantri Didi Kitchen, which provides free food to the needy. At present, the state has about 4,185 community kitchens in as many Panchayats, with SRLM providing Rs 20,000 each to SHGs running these centres. The Didi helpline, a telephonic helpline initiated by Jharkhand SRLM, is open 24 hours to help migrant labourers by providing them verified information. It enables them to provide their data to state authorities to help evacuate them from different states, back to Jharkhand.

Contribution of J&K Rural Livelihood Mission (JKRLM) in Combating COVID-19

Keeping in view the objective of dealing with distress situation COVID-19 pandemic, and to provide relief to the affected, Jammu and Kashmir Rural Livelihood Mission (JKRLM) did its bid and carried- out following interventions:

(i) JKSRLM, across blocks created awareness amongst the SHGs members, on prevention of COVID -19. The SHG members are made aware on importance of hand washing with soap, physical distancing, quarantine, avoiding of unnecessary travel etc. they have also made aware of the emergency cell/phone number issued by the district administrations. The awareness was provided at the Cluster Federation level, which inturn provided the awareness at the Village Organizations at the village level. The awareness drive was part of concerted efforts by different departments which complemented in making people conscious about the various simple necessary steps at the household level to break the chain of the pandemic.

(ii) The initial online training was organized by DAY-NRLM, National Mission Management Unit (NMMU) in which around 250 participants from J&K participated. The 250 facilitated behavior change management trainings to about 73,000 SHGs members, whom further trained through word of mouth in their vicinity 289,000 SHG members across 96 undivided blocks under Umeed, JKRLM.

(iii) During the lock down period, the households who have sole income based daily labour have become the most impacted. To ensure the food security, in few blocks, the SHGs from their own resources collected ration items and distributed among the needy and poor households. A kit consisting of rice, edible oil, pulses were distributed among the poor households.

(iv) 3,000 bottles of hand sanitizers with 100 ml quantity in each have also been produced so far by the SHGs.

(v) Amid fast spreading COVID-19, SHG women from JKRLM started making masks in an effort to help the general public. As the J&K is facing dearth of masks in the wake of COVID-19 outbreak, the SHG members associated with JKSRLM have stepped up to fill the void and contributed for the noble cause. The first consignment of 12,200 masks were made available within 36 hours and has been handed over to the Districts Administration. SHG promoted by JKSRLM have produced so far 11,31,857 masks which is stitched by the SHGs members. So far 1,100 SHGs have been engaged in producing the masks. Through JKSRLM facilitation, the SHGs have sold the masks to the Govt. administration and the Sri Mata Vaishno Devi Shrine Board. The SHGs have made a sale of Rs 84,17,157; out of which the SHG have received the Rs 58,02,671 into their accounts; whereas Rs 26,14,486 is pending with the district administration.

The District wise details of payments and balance given below:

Sl. No.	***District***	***Payment made to SHG***	***Vendor***	***Sl. No.***	***District***	***Payments Pending***	***Vendor***
1.	Jammu	75250	Govt admin	1.	Reasi	961490	Govt admin
2.	Reasi	64645	Sri Mata Vishno	2.	Shopian	21906	Govt admin
3.	Kishtwar	803000	Govt admin	3.	Pulwama	89896	Govt admin
4.	Pulwama	269688	Govt admin	4.	Kulgam	600000	Govt admin
5.	Kulgam	450000	Govt admin	5.	Kupwara	345914	Govt admin
6.	Kupwara	2809296	Govt admin	6.	Bandipora	249460	Govt admin
7.	Bandipora	682934	Govt admin	7.	Srinagar	269250	Govt admin
8.	Srinagar	76500	Govt admin	8.	Ganderbal	76570	Govt admin
9.	Anantnag	391374	Govt admin	9.	Anantnag	726714	Govt admin
10.	Baramulla	179984	Govt admin	10.	Baramulla	734384	Govt admin
	Total	5802671			Total	2614486	

In many other states, SHG members engaged as BC Sakhi (banking correspondent agents) help home-delivered the Centre's financial relief packages for the rural community facing socio-economic distress, pensioners, and those who are dependent on the Mahatma Gandhi National Rural Employment Guarantee Act.

The motivated, enthusiastic and committed approximately 690 lakh women members of around 63 lakh Self Help Groups (SHGs) across the country formed have always contributed in addressing economic and social needs that have emerged at the community level. These women are engaged in livelihoods activities, bringing social change through awareness generation, leading movements and responding during natural calamities. During the on-going crisis also, SHG members have emerged as community warriors by contributing in every possible way to contain the spread of COVID-19.

The SHG network across the country was made aware of the various aspects of the disease including the need to maintain personal hygiene, social distancing etc. through Audio Visual (AV) IEC material and advisories developed by Health Ministry which were circulated to all State Rural Livelihoods Missions (SRLMs). All such information, along with materials developed by the state governments, is being used by the SRLMs to ensure that the correct message is communicated to the community about all required precautions. The SRLM staff and SHGs members are creating awareness in the local communities by various means like telephone calls, wall writings, pamphlets/fliers etc. Social media is also being used extensively.

Sustaining their livelihoods through socially responsive contributions in promoting safe hygiene practices within their respective communities, these SHG women have been fighting the COVID-19 outbreak with utmost dedication and devotion. Through many similar responsible collective actions organized across the nation, marginalised and vulnerable women of these communities have played a significant role in the war against Coronavirus while being empowered both socially and economically.

Women collectives stepped up to promote hand hygiene in their communities with affordable hand Sanitizers. The micro-enterprises supported by DAY-NRLM have taken up the production of hand sanitisers and hand wash products to ensure the availability in rural areas. 900 SHG enterprises in 9 States have produced 1.15 lakh litres of sanitisers with the production in the three States of Tamil Nadu, Madhya Pradesh and Andhra Pradesh exceeding 25,000 litres each. Around 900 SHG enterprises located across the states of Andhra Pradesh, Himachal Pradesh, Jharkhand, Kerala, Manipur, Madhya Pradesh, Nagaland, Tamil Nadu, Uttar Pradesh and Mizoram are producing sanitizers to feed soaring demand. Following guidelines proposed by World Health Organization (WHO), a well-measured mix of four ingredients has been used to develop these sanitizers in Jharkhand. The sanitizer has been developed using alcohol (72%), distilled water (13%), glycerin (13%) and basil (2%). For their medicinal effects, lemon grass or basil are being added to the hand sanitizer to increase its effectiveness in destroying the virus. Priced modestly at Rs. 30/- per 100 ml bottle of sanitizer, they are being made available to the general public, hospitals and police stations.

Some SHGs have also been selling liquid soaps to guarantee safe hand hygiene. SHG units located in the states of Andhra Pradesh, Chhattisgarh, Madhya Pradesh, Maharashtra, Mizoram, Nagaland, Tamil Nadu have also been able to produce 50,000 litres of hand-washing products.

SHG volunteers are playing their role in ensuring that people maintain social distancing in markets, PDS shops etc. In Tamil Nadu, two volunteers of SHGs are assigned to each PDS shop. They are provided gloves, masks and sanitisers and they ensure that people in the queue maintain adequate distance.

Factors Enabling SHGs to Contribute in Combating COVID-19

Here are four main reasons why SHGs have been able to play an important role in serving the rural poor amidst COVID-19:

(i) First, they have a better understanding of local communities, and in times of crises, have immediate access on the ground.

(ii) Second, they serve as an integral community communication channel, help reach the last mile, and are trusted by local communities.

(iii) Third, they can provide short- and medium-term social and economic protection, serving as a critical conduit for providing relief to the most vulnerable.

(iv) Fourth, they quickly set up the production of relevant items using their well-honed skills, and put to use village distribution and supply chains.

Conclusion

As we celebrate and acknowledge their contributions in tackling the coronavirus pandemic, we must continue to strengthen them, and replicate the model across the country. They must be given a requisite economic and social empowerment. Governments and society must recognise that effective emergency response and the social and economic protection of the most vulnerable is critically dependent on institutions like SHGs.

References

Documents of World Bank accessed from https://www.worldbank.org/

Documents of the Ministry of Rural Development accessed from https://rural.nic.in/

Documents of Deendayal Antyodaya Yojana- National Rural Livelihoods Mission accessed from https://aajeevika.gov.in/

Various articles of the Hindustan Times accessed from https://www.hindustantimes.com/

Reports of Jammu & Kashmir Rural Livelihood Mission (JKRLM)

Data from field visit

Chapter - 12

Impact of COVID-19 on Rural Livelihoods: A Sociological Study of Telangana

— *Mr. Sreeramulu Gosikonda*

Introduction

COVID-19 is an infectious disease caused by the newly discovered Corona Virus. This new virus and disease were found in Wuhan city, China, in December 2019 whereas the first case in India was reported in January 2020. The spread of COVID-19 in India hit the lives of people in all of its states, where the majority of the workforce engaged in the unorganized sector in general and rural livelihoods in particular. To stop the spread of the virus, the Government of India strictly implemented the nationwide lockdown in four phases that started on 25.03.2020 and ended on 31.05.2020. This nationwide lockdown ceased interstate transportation by excluding essential goods and commodities. The majority of the states took proper steps to supply essentials for the people. However, it has severely affected lives and livelihoods across rural India during the pandemic. More than half of the workforce in the country depends on agriculture and allied sectors. Around 85% of farmers in India are small and marginal farmers, who hold less than two hectares of land. Besides, around 14 million people depend on fisheries for their livelihood directly and indirectly. Hence, the Ministry of Home Affairs, Government of India issued guidelines on 15.04.2020 to exempt agriculture and allied sectors from lockdown restrictions. It also allowed the operation of various works under the Mahatma Gandhi National Rural Employment Guarantee Scheme (MGNREGS).

Telangana is the 12th largest state in India with an area of 112.08 lakh hectares, of which about 60% of it is arable. Agriculture plays a vital role in the economy of the State in which around 55.5 % of its population is dependent on farm activity for livelihoods. The marginal holdings (less than 1 hectare) and smallholdings (1 to 2 hectares) of the state are 62% and 24% respectively, which constitute about 86% of total agricultural holdings in the State. It indicates that the majority of the population depends on agriculture for their livelihood with little income generated from their smallholdings. Agriculture comes under the primary sector which includes agriculture, horticulture, animal husbandry, and fisheries.

Objectives and Methodology

The present chapter "*Impact of Lockdown on Rural Livelihoods: A Sociological Analysis from Telangana State*" aims to find out the employment problems of rural people during the period of lockdown that implemented by both central and state governments. It captures the responses of rural people on their economic loss due to lockdown.

The present paper is based on both primary and secondary sources. The researcher attended a marriage on 20.03.2020 at his native place and stuck there for almost two months due to the nationwide lockdown. The critical situation of people belong to his village attracted the researcher to carry out empirical research. Though the researcher had the interest to carry out the study at any other village, there was no chance to do so as no village allowed people from other places. Hence, the Rampur village of Huzurabad Mandal in Karimnagar District was selected by the researcher. The village locates 3 km away from Huzurabad town. Most of the people go to the town daily for various purposes ranging from education to employment. However, the majority of the working people in general and women, in particular, depend on agriculture and allied sectors. For exploring the impact of lockdown on rural livelihoods, an empirical study was conducted by the researcher. Around 50 respondents, who engage in different occupations, were interviewed by the researcher by employing a structured interview schedule. The researcher adopted a convenience sampling technique to identify respondents in the village. All the precautious measurements such as physical distance, wearing a face mask, hand wash, etc. were followed by the researcher while conducting interviews with the respondents.

Findings

The Government of Telangana implemented '*Janata Curfew*' from 22.03.2020 and extended the lockdown till 31.05.2020 as per the guidelines given by the Government of India. All the markets, various types of shops, wine/liquor shops, and temples were closed. All marriages, religious festivals, ceremonies, and *jataras* were stopped. Even the operation of public and private transport vehicles banned and strict rules were implemented on the movement of people except for essentials things such as rice, Kirana provisions, vegetables, milk, medicine, etc. to control the spread of the Coronavirus. However, the lockdown in rural Telanganawounded the day-to-day life and economy in the countryside.

Impact of Lockdown on Rural Livelihoods

The study captured the economic impact of the nationwide lockdown on rural people. The study noticed that lockdown influenced rural livelihoods adversely. Though rural people faced multiple problems, majority of the people suffered from financial problems.

Identification of Rural Livelihoods

The researcher identified that working people engaged in diverse fields of occupation. Those are self-employment, farming, owning and operating tractors and harvesters, weaving, agricultural labour, manual labour, fishery, dairy, toddy tapping, masonry, carpentry, jewel-making, sheep/goat rearing, drum beating, *purohit* (priesthood), stone cutting, beedi making, hairdressing, washing, tailoring, painting, salesmen and other workers in cloth stores and other shops at Huzurabad, teaching in government schools/colleges, teaching in private schools/colleges at Huzurabad and Jammikunta and engage in various business activities at Huzurabad such as running boutique shops, photo studios, winding works, rexine works, refrigerator shops, running chits, workshops of engineering works and steel almirahs, etc. The researcher further identified that owning and running of *MeeSeva* center, electrician, owning mineral water plant and supplying mineral water within the village and/or in Huzurabad town, running different types of shops such as Kirana shop, chicken shop, cycle shop, etc., cooking at various types of functions/events/celebrations, running evening hotels, bangle sellers, broom sellers, auto-rickshaw drivers, ice cream vendors, dry fish sellers, seasonal fruit vendors, sweet vendors and doll sellers at *Jataras*, owning a flour mill, owning a tent house, RMP Doctor, dish operator, DTH service provider, and petty business are part of self-employment livelihoods in the village.

Economic Impact of Lockdown on Rural People

The study noticed that majority of the rural livelihoods were affected due to lockdown. However, there is no such negative impact of lockdown on

Kirana shops, chicken centers, cable operators, DTH service providers, and toddy tappers in the village. All households depended on local Kirana shops for getting groceries as nobody willing to go Huzurabad. Of course, the owners of Kirana shops charged high rates for essential goods as they purchased them at higher rates from the wholesale shops at Huzurabad. The supply of essential goods was not up to the mark due to the restrictions in both intra and interstate transports. There was no demand for chicken in January and February, 2020 as people believed that the virus would spread through birds and animals. Some of the poultry farmers distributed hens free of cost to the people as there was no demand in the market. Even some of the farmers left the chicks without rearing as they thought of wastage of their investment. Later on, the Telangana Poultry Association mentioned it very clear that immunity power would be increased by eating eggs and chicken which is an essential element to face the Coronavirus. Hence, during the lockdown period, people increased the consumption of eggs and chicken for improving their immunity power to fight against the virus. Further, there was a huge demand for television as all of the family members stayed at home only and watched it for passing time to avoid boring. Besides, toddy (palm wine) was preferred by many of the people as the liquor shops were closed due to lockdown.

Agriculture and Allied Sectors

It is observed from the field that the main crop of the village is paddy, in which the majority of the farmers are marginal and small farmers. March and April are the main harvesting seasons of paddy crop (*rabi)*. As the agricultural markets were closed, the farmers were at crossroads. Then the Government of Telangana allowed IKP Centres and rice millers to procure paddy produce from the farmers directly from their fields. However, farmers in the village alleged that rice millers depreciated the weight of paddy in the name of wastage, moisture, and low quality of the crop. The following narration describes how paddy farmers got financial loss during the lockdown period.

> Mr. Swamy Reddy, a paddy farmer said that he got produced about 160 bags of 40 kg each in his 3 acres of land. He sold 120 bags of BPT-5204 to the seed plant and the remaining 40 bags of MTU-1010 to the IKP Centre. The seed plant depreciated 2 kg per bag whereas the IKP centredepreciated 1kg per bag in the name of chaffy grain and dust & dirt. He was worried that he lost around Rs. 5294 because of this exploitation by the rice millers during the pandemic (MSP: BPT-5204@1900 per quintal; 120 bags x2 kg=240 kg x Rs.19=Rs. 4560

and MSP: MTU-1010@1835 per quintal: 40 bags x 1kg=40 kg x Rs. 18.35= Rs. 734).

The study noticed that the farmers who cultivated vegetables, flowers, and fruits suffered a lot. The farmers were not able to sell their vegetables at Huzurabad due to a lack of transport facilities and restrictions in the market area. Hence, they sold their vegetables within the village by going streets at lower prices. The next one is that there is no market for flowers as functions were restricted, marriages were postponed and temples were closed. Generally, many marriages are held in Telangana from March *to May, which is also the main season for flower crops. Hence, marriages have a positive impact on the income of flower farmers. The farmers who cultivate Lilly and Jasmine are hit by severe losses. The farmers who cultivate watermelon sold them in villages by hiring a tractor at lower prices. Even the onion farmers visited villages by hiring tractor and sold their produce at cheaper rates.* In this way, all types of farmers witnessed the immediate loss of income in addition to the indebtedness. The following narration of a female farmer explains how the vegetable farmers suffered economically during the period of lockdown.

> Mrs. Ambakka, a vegetable vendor and who has a vehicle for that purpose said that there was no market for the vegetables for the previous two months. She felt that the yield was optimum in her fields but there were no customers to buy. She added that the middlemen asked them to sell okra (ladies' fingers) and tomato at Rs.2 per kg so that they dumped in the market. On the whole, they got a loss of around Rs. 15000 during this pandemic. She worried that they were facing economic problems as they lifted chits and took vehicle loans, in which they have to repay weekly/monthly without fail.

It is evident from the field that even the fisherman did not have any demand as restrictions were imposed both in markets and to entry other villages. As all the activities were stopped due to the lockdown, all types of agricultural laborers did not get any work in the fields. The agricultural laborers who depend completely on agriculture for their livelihood became penniless. In this way, all agricultural laborers witnessed dire poverty due to the pandemic and prone to take debts from others to meet their daily expenses during this period. The study noticed that most of the agricultural laborers tried to adjust and manage their families with the support given by the government during the lockdown period.

> Mrs. Saraswathi, an agricultural laborer said that she could engage in plucking jasmine during the marriage season, where she could get

Rs. 150 per day. But due to lockdown, there was no market for the jasmines and the farmer stopped all the operations of jasmine cultivation. She could also send agricultural laborers to other villages in autos for harvesting of various crops such as picking cotton, plucking red chili, cutting maize, etc., where she could get Rs. 300 per day from the farmer. Besides, she used to go along with his brother to assist him while he was cooking for different types of parties and functions. She felt that she lost all these works and unable to run her family due to the lockdown. Hence, she borrowed Rs. 5000 from her neighbours.

The study also witnessed that all the enrolled workers of the MGNREGS did not get any work during the first month of lockdown as it was stopped by the government.

Non-Agriculture Sectors

The study found that around 80 members were working in the Bapuji Handloom Weavers' Co-operative Society, which is located in the village. The society was closed due to the lockdown. Hence, all workers of society lost their livelihood. Though they draw low wages, they lost their bread and lead a pitiable life.

Mr. K. Sadanandam, a weaver said that he could earn around Rs. 4000 per month by weaving towels in the society. But he did not have any work and lost around Rs. 8000 for these two months due to lockdown. Even the yarn was not sufficient in society due to a lack of transport facilities. Hence, he took borrow Rs. 5000 from his relatives to meet the expenses during the period of lockdown.

All the self-employed people were unable to perform any work during the lockdown period. All the auto drivers, dry fish venders, bangle sellers, broom sellers, ice cream vendors, fruit sellers, painters, tailors, vegetable vendors, electricians, doll sellers, etc. have stayed at home without any economic activity.

Mr. Bhaskar, an ice cream vendor cum mango seller said that he did not have any from February, 2020. He said that he could earn around Rs. 500 daily by selling ice creams in villages and Rs. 30000 by selling mangoes for the whole season. He felt that this loss hit his family in all aspects. He felt that because of the lockdown, his family was witnessing severe economic loss, which cannot be bringing back again.

It is evident from the field that some of the men were working in different types of shops at Huzurabad. As the shops were closed, they lost their employment for two months. Moreover, they expressed a doubt that the shop owners might not continue them in the same job as they might face financial problems in running their shop itself due to lockdown.

> Mr. Ramesh, a salesman at the Cloth store in Huzurabad said that his salary was Rs. 15000 per month. But he did not get any salary for the last two months. He felt stress as he was unable to manage his family due to lockdown. He added that they have to repay all the debts that took from SHG and other private chits.

Further, the study observed that working people who depend not only on traditional occupations such as carpenters, gold smiths, barbers, washer men, etc. but also on modern occupations such as electric and motor winding works, boutique shops, refrigerator shops, steel almirah shops, business, etc. did not have any work and witnessed economic loss during the period of lockdown. It is also evident from the field that the traditional village drummers lost their employment due to restrictions on all types of ceremonies.

Impact of Postponement of Marriages on Rural Livelihoods

To stop the spread of the novel coronavirus, all functions related to human life right from birthday celebrations to death formalities were restricted and limited to family only. In other words, all types of social gatherings were banned. As all the marriages and private functions were not allowed by the government, parents postponed marriages of their children. Though marriage event is related to two families, it has positive impact on the livelihoods of priests, photographers, farmers that cultivate flowers and/or vegetables, tailors, owners of tent houses, owners of chicken/mutton centers, cooks, etc. The marriage functions need priests for performing poojas, which is very essential in getting done marriage between bride and bridegroom. Garments play a vital role in marriages where tailors services are needed. They also require photographers and videographers for recording sweet memories of the event. As marriage is a great event in one's life, they invite their near and dear and arrange for lunch/dinner with veg and/or non-veg. The services of cook/s are required for cooking different varieties of food items and dishes. Finally, various types of tent house materials are neededfor not only providing seating accommodation to all the attendees but also preparing andcatering food.

> Mr. V. Surendar, a priest said that it was the main season for him to perform poojas. He said that he missed several marriages and other religious/cultural functions where he could earn around Rs. 50,000 for these two months of lockdown.

Ch. Ramulu, the owner of Tent House said that they did not get any order for the tent house except deaths which have very limited orders. He felt that this was the main season for the tent house where a lot of marriages and other functions took place. He worried that they would have gained around Rs. 2 lakh in these two months if the lockdown was not there.

In this way, the postponement of marriages hit seriously the livelihoods of priests, photographers, horticulture farmers, tailors, owners of tent houses and cooks in the village.

Organized Sector

The study noticed that very few people belong to the village were working in the organized sector. Among them, most of the people are private school teachers and private college lecturers whereas very few people are government school teachers. The Government of Telangana has announced to give 50% of the salary to all the government employees including government teachers due to the critical economic condition of the state that was resulted by the lockdown. However, the government can pay the remaining salary to all its employees once the economic condition of the state sets right. But the economic situation of the teachers and lecturers who work in private schools and colleges was so pathetic. Despite their salaries are very less when compared to government teachers, they did not get a salary for three months from March to May, 2020. Hence, the private school teachers and private college lecturers were in the frontline among the organized sector employees who witnessed the worst conditions in their life during the period of pandemic.

Miss. Sravanthi, an unmarried teacher said that the school management did not give a salary for May month due to summer vacation. Hence, she did not get a salary for 3 months i.e. from March to May, 2020, which worth Rs. 13,500. Her mother was an agricultural laborer and her father was no more. She did not have any hope to lead their family as both of them did not have any work. She added that she was waiting for opening school to get employment but expressed her doubt whether the management continues her in the job or not.

Mr. Mruthyunjay, an experienced private school teacher said that the management did not pay the salaries for the lockdown period, though the Government insisted upon the regular payment of the salaries to all private employees. The management said that they did not collect the fee from the parents as the schools were closed without conducting final examinations. Generally, parents pay fees to private schools before final examinations. Besides, the government insisted upon not forcing anyone to collect school fees. He felt that private school teachers don't demand management for salaries due to job insecurity. Hence, most of the private teachers engage in other works as they were hopeless in their jobs due to various reasons.

The above responses reflect the painful situation of private school teachers, which has not ended with the lockdown. In fact, they have to face the same critical economic situation till reopening of schools/colleges. Hence, there is a need to have attention of government/s to look into the financial issues of private teachers/lecturers.

Support from the Government and Other Agencies

The Government of Telangana implemented the rules given by the Government of India to ensure food security and financial support during the lockdown period. The study captured that those who have a white ration card, the government supplied 12kg rice per person through PDS shops and transferred an amount Rs. 1500 per household into their bank account directly. However, few of the families recognized that amount had not been credited into their accounts. Finally, they received an amount from the post office. It is observed from the field that an amount of Rs. 500, which was a central government aid under Pradhan Mantri Garib Kalyan Yojana, was not received by the majority of the people in the village.

Besides, the support given by the Government of Telangana, the auto drivers, and weavers received groceries from different sources. The local minister distributed 25 kg of rice with essential goods to all the auto drivers belong to the village. The Padmashali Officials and Professionals Association (POPA) of Huzurabad distributed 10 kg rice with essential goods to all the weavers and other workers belong to the Bapuji Handloom Weavers' Co-operative Society, Rampur.

The study observed that all the respondents received ration (rice) and cash from the government. The majority of them expressed that the government support would not enough to lead their family but tried to adjust with that help as there was no other way to deal with this critical situation. Most of the people took debts from their relatives and friends to pay installments in SHGs. All the owners of private chits did not collect money for two months from their customers. However, most of the women were ready to take loans from the SHGs to revive their economic condition after lifting the lockdown.

Conclusion

The study noticed that as Curfew and Lockdown are new to the rural people, the majority of them were not ready to move out of their home. It is evident from the field that during the lockdown period, all the farmers witnessed economic loss, which impacts on their investment in the cultivation of the coming crop. Besides, few of the farmers were unable to sell their perishable items such as vegetables and fruits, where they experienced psychological stress. Though agricultural activities were allowed after one month of the lockdown, maintaining physical distance is a major challenge in working places. Hence, the majority of the people were not engaged in any activity until the lockdown is lifted. It is observed from the field that many of the people did not have money even to meet their daily needs so that they were prone to take debts.

In this way, the lockdown harms the rural people in general and farmers, agricultural laborers, weavers, self-employed people, workers in organized & unorganized sectors, and private teachers/lecturers. During the lockdown period, there was a serious setback in rural economic activities which cannot be recovered immediately. Though it takes a long time to resettle the rural economy, it needs meticulous policies. Hence, it is suggested that the government should sanction loans to all the working people with zero interest to retain and sustain their livelihoods. Both central and state governments should give much priority for the revival of the rural economy in their Post-Corona plans that can create confidence among the rural people to lead a comfortable life. Then only the rural people can overcome both psychological and economic stress with a ray of hope. Otherwise, there will be more chances to lead either rural unrest or increase migration from rural to urban areas. The study also appeals thatthe government should take appropriate measures to lead a dignified life by private teachers/lecturers.

References

http://ecostat.telangana.gov.in/PDF/PUBLICATIONS/Statistical_Year_Book_2016.pdf

https://www.telangana.gov.in/PDFDocuments/Statistical-Year-Book-2017.pdf

http://www.tsdps.telangana.gov.in/downloads/Socio-Economic-Outlook-2018.pdf

http://agricoop.gov.in/sites/default/files/agristatglance2017.pdf

https://www.worldbank.org/content/dam/Worldbank/document/SAR/SO.pdf

https://www.orfonline.org/expert-speak/impact-covid19-rural-lives-livelihoods-india-64889/

https://www.mssrf.org/content/livelihoods-smallholder-farmers-engaged-floriculture-tamil-nadu

https://link.springer.com/chapter/10.1007/978-3-030-14409-8_3

https://www.ifpri.org/blog/addressing-COVID-19-impacts-agriculture-food-security-and-livelihoods-india

https://diplomatist.com/2020/04/30/impact-of-COVID-19-on-rural-india/

https://www.thehindubusinessline.com/opinion/protecting-rural-livelihoods-under-COVID-19/article31508089.ece#

https://www.cbgaindia.org/blog/impact-COVID-19-rural-areas-andhra-pradesh-governments-response/

https://www.thehindubusinessline.com/news/national/COVID-19-lockdown-cripple-rural-life-economy-in-telangana/article31493442.ece

https://telanganatoday.com/telangana-govt-eases-out-lockdown-in-rural-areas-allows-informal-industries-to-function

Chapter - 13

Impact of COVID-19 on Rural Education in India

— *Dr. Rajeev Bansal*

Introduction

Majority of India lives in villages and rural education in India is of utmost importance. Education is the most important tool for social, economic and political transformation and a key instrument for building an equitable society. A well-educated population, equipped with the relevant knowledge, attitudes and skills is essential for economic and social development in the twenty-first century. Education at the elementary level serves as the catalyst in the growth of a child from being a novice to become a person with the knowledge and skills required for him to live in the society. Education, being a social institution serving the needs of society, is indispensable for a society to survive and thrive. It is required not only to be comprehensive, sustainable, but also must continuously evolve to meet the challenges of the fast-changing and unpredictable globalized world. Quality and access to education is the major concern in rural schools as there are fewer committed teachers, lack of proper text books and learning material in the schools. Though Government schools exist, but when compared to private schools then quality is a major issue. Majority of people living in villages have understood the importance of education and know that it is the only way to get rid of poverty but due to lack of money they are not able to send their children to private schools and hence depend upon government schools for education.More than 24 million children aged between 3-5 years lack essential skills required to thrive in school; 25 million primary school children lack age-appropriate learning competencies. The Indian government spends 4.6 percent of its GDP on education, lower than sub-Saharan countries like Kenya, Togo and Zimbabwe.

Rural Education in India

In rural areas, the parents prefer to take their children to farms telling them that since they don't have to go to schools, they must help them in harvesting crops. Usually, in March, most of the farmers were occupied harvesting crops and sowing for the next season. This affects the education of children as well. Parents take their children to farms telling them that since they don't have to go to schools, they must help them in harvesting crops. This helps them get an extra harvest for the day.The facts and figures present a grim picture on the canvas of rural education in India.

Status in Reports

- As per the report tabled by the Ministry of Human Resource Development in the Lok Sabha in 2020, the reasons for children dropping out of school include poverty or economic reasons, poor health, a child too young to be attending school is needed for help in domestic work.
- As per the Annual Status of Education Report, 2018, no more than 2.8 percent of children are out of school in India, the first time the figure has fallen below 3 percent, bringing the total school enrolment to a record 97.2 percent. However, as per the same report, such improvements mask latent issues in the country's rural school network, where numeracy and literacy standards remain sub-par, and in many instances, lower than standards recorded 10 years ago in 2008.

Enrollment

India has 1.4 million schools, 2.01 million children enrolled in government schools from Standard 1-8 and an additional 3.8 million children enrolled in Standard 9-10, according to the UDISE report on school education in India, 2016-2017. Approximately 29% of India's population are children, and 19.29 % is in the age group of 6-14 years. This group is legally entitled to education under the Right to Education (RTE) Act, 2009.

Expenditure

In the Union budget 2017-18, the Finance Minister announced an allocation of Rs 72,394 crore compared to Rs 68,963 crore for last year, which is a 4.9 percent increase in the education budget out of which approx. 30 percent is spent on higher education. Out of the remaining funds, a meagre amount is spent on education in rural India as a result of which more than half of

India's population is left uneducated. The state and central governments are trying to tackle these issues by pumping almost Rs 310 billion (approx. $5.7 billion) into improving rural school infrastructure and recruiting teachers.

Education Envisaged in SDGs

The Goal 4 of SDGS laying emphasis on Quality Educations specifies to ***Ensure inclusive and equitable quality education and promote lifelong opportunity for all.*** The specific targets of this goal relating with elementary education mention that:

4.1 By 2030, ensure that all girls and boys complete free, equitable and quality primary and secondary education leading to relevant and effective learning outcomes

4.2 By 2030, ensure that all girls and boys have access to quality early childhood development, care and pre-primary education so that they are ready for primary education

The future course of action and strategy for elementary education has to be designed and formulated in the above context to achieve the targets within the timeline.

COVID-19 & Rural Education

The lockdown to contain spread of COVID-19 has resulted into an interruption to learning activity of school going children. And in the case of dropouts, it was the final straw for at-risk children who struggled to get an education at the best of times. The children have been experiencing a global learning crisis, as many students were in school, but were not learning the fundamental skills needed for life. The UN Policy Brief (August 2020) observed that the COVID-19 pandemic has created the largest disruption of education systems in history, affecting nearly 1.6 billion learners in more than 190 countries and all continents. Closures of schools and other learning spaces have impacted 94 percent of the world's student population, up to 99 percent in low and lower-middle income countries.

ICT Status in Rural India

The status of information, communication and technology has been broadly categorized in two major sections in context of rural education scenario-

(i) **Digital Literacy:** The factual position on account of computer literacy at the elementary level can be assessed that

- Most of the children and teachers haven't even heard about the online classes.
- It is not possible to make Zoom or Webex or Google Meet calls to children in rural and tribal areas. Teachers, as well as the children, are used to the chalk and board method.
- It does not make sense to send them notes or videos through WhatsApp or voice recordings.
- Another person from Barka Gaon village in Muzaffarpur, Bihar quoted that he had a smartphone, but he did not know how to teach children through it.
- There exist many loopholes when it comes to educating children living in rural areas virtually. It is heartening that few are studying, rest are playing

(ii) Internet Usage: The status of internet usage in terms of its knowledge, availability and usage at the level of primary and middle schools in rural India highlight that:

- With an estimated population of 918 million as per the 2011 census, there are only 186 million Internet users in rural India.
- As per the Internet and Mobile Association of India (IAMAI) report, 70% of the rural population does not access the internet actively.
- There is a wide gap in internet usage in urban and rural India. While internet penetration in urban India is about 64.85 percent, it's just 20.26 percent in rural areas.
- As per the IAMAI report, only 7% of those living in rural India use the Internet for educational purposes.
- As per the Gaon Connection survey conducted in 2019, of the 18,267 people who were interviewed, 80% used internet through various means.

Impact of COVID-19 on Rural Education and Challenges

The education disruption has ripple effects beyond the education sector and will continue to have such overarching effects in the times to come. Closures of educational institutions stagnate the provision of essential services to children and communities, including access to nutritious food, affect the ability of many parents to work and increase risks of violence against women and girls. The Education sector has come on a hold amid the COVID-19 lockdown and children in rural India have suffered the most. The school education system portrays a dismal picture. There are innumerable village level elementary schools under the Sarva Shiksha Abhiyan scheme, catering to the below-poverty-level sections of society. A majority of children attend village elementary and primary schools. Structure of schooling and learning, including teaching and assessment methodologies, was the first to be affected by these closures. The students missed opportunities for learning besides effect on the decrease of the employment rate- a bigger concern. The impact of COVID-19 can be understood in the succeeding text:

(i) Academic Loss:

- State governments have shut down schools and colleges temporarily as a measure to contain the spread with no certainty when they will reopen. It is a crucial time for the education sector as the closures not only have a short-term impact on the continuity of learning for more than 285 million young learners in India.
- Social distancing and severe lockdowns across the globe has forced people to find innovative ways to do their routine jobs.
- One of the first measures taken by the Indian Government was to close the educational institutions for the safety of students, teachers, and their families. The steps were taken by the government were necessary and brought in the right direction to stop the further spread of the virus in the country.
- The teachers are impacted significantly at the workplace andprofessionally. All educational institutions may not have strategies for the teachingcontinuity activity and temporary contracts may be terminated.
- The non-teaching staff constitutes the most vulnerable sector in terms of possible reduction in the number of jobs.
- Further, there is possible financial curtailment due to the cancellation of fees or reduction in student enrollment. A huge disruptor of the functions of temporary termination of face- to- face activities in schools etc.
- There is a decline in demand in the short term and a spike in the next academic year. The shutdown of the education institutions has led to many apprehensions among the students and teaching fraternity, therefore, it is too early to estimate the future profile of the education offer.
- The extended disrupted education disengaged students from the learning process will result into comparative disadvantage

in learning results. It further adversely affected academic, socio-economic, students with special/diverse educational needs or persons with disabilities in terms of learning challenges with new remote learning strategies.

- The area of concern in this phase of the crisis on children and youth in terms of losses in learning, increased dropout rates and children missing their most important meal of the day.

Digital Illiteracy and Academic Loss: Case Study of Uttar Pradesh

State Government advised teachers to send educational content through WhatsApp groups, radio and community radios. It was a good idea, but hardly anyone one bothered to think about practical problems like internet connectivity, the number of active internet users and data packs available to the guardians and students in the rural pockets. But their effectiveness is questionable. There are hardly people in the villages having radio, whereas not even 10% would be aware of the radio lectures.

Many teachers had created WhatsApp groups and added parents. It is hard to believe that no one replied to those messages. Many teachers keep motivating parents for using the internet for educational purposes, but there is a lack of awareness. Only those children whose parents are educated are managing to study during this lockdown. A primary school teacher from Lakauda village in Suratganj block of Uttar Pradesh's Barabanki district admitted of sending recorded audio lectures to the children but not many have smartphones and hence they cannot access this content. "All the kids are not getting the benefit of this initiative," reported a primary school teacher, Khairabad village in Uttar Pradesh's Sitapur district. "Of the 223 students, only 20-25 are in touch through WhatsApp. Only those studying in Class 4 and 5 manage to contact us," said a primary school teacher from Hasuri Ausanpur village, Siddhrathnagar district, Uttar Pradesh.

It does not matter if they have smartphones or not, these children are going to learn only when their parents are aware. Not many families in rural areas have smartphones. Those who do, they don't necessarily have the internet packs.

(ii) Digital Divide:

- Gradually, the system is getting accustomed to the situation. Distance classes or through dedicated TV channels or using various online platforms, have been started in many institutions, however, difficult to sayhow far it has been successful.

- A few students are used to having online chats on their smartphones. Some students in rural areas cannot connect, mainly due to poor internet connectivity in their hometowns.
- There comes the aspect of the digital divide: most poor students do not have access to smartphones, and even if they do, the net connectivity is poor and content is often not available in vernacular languages. This gives rise to discrimination in access to education.
- Today many schools in urban areas are having online classes, while the majority of rural schools do not. Very young children are not able to learn through online processes as they can neither handle computers nor mobile phones. In rural households, there is no computer, and in many, children are not allowed smartphones as well. Both these problems exist regardless of class. Therefore, the digital divide at the school level leads to a gap between the haves and have-nots.
- Examinations have either been postponed, cancelled or students have been promoted to next classes on the basis of previous assessment but without any examination. Cancelling annual exams will only weaken the foundations of the students.

Responses

The challenges as discussed previously deserve to be converted into opportunity for the promising future of learning and the changes in modes of delivering quality education to be accelerated for the objective of leaving no one behind.

(i) **Policy and Institutional Responses:** In terms of policy responses, States have limited themselves to three areas viz. (a) administrative measures to safeguard the operation of the system; (b) financial resources; and (c) the provision of infrastructure to continue learning activities. Besides this, institutional responses have covered strictly on the health front, adjustment of academic calendars, research and development contribution to mitigate the pandemic, guarantee of continuity of teaching activities through distance education and technological resources as well as socio-emotional support to the teaching learning community.

(ii) **Leveraging digital Technology Transforming Education:** Shagun, an integrated Online junction for school education, one of world's largest system of its kind to improve school education launched. New national Curriculum & Pedagogical Framework for school education, teachers education and early childhood stage to prepare them as per global benchmarks. Multi-mode access to education through online platforms to benefit nearly 25 crore school children. DIKSHA Portal providing quality e-content for school education and QR coded energized textbooks. Shiksha Vani providing extensive use of Radio, community radio and CBSE podcast launched for the benefit of students.

(iii) **Expanding Edutech Platforms Amidst Lockdown:** The Central Govt. devised policies to promote students from Class I to Class VIII to next class, students of Class IX and Class XI to be promoted on the basis of internal assessment, SWAYAM 2.0 launched to facilitate online degree programmes by top ranking universities, 28 online courses for Class XI & XII, 90,000 students enrolled till 16th May, 2020. Under E-Pathshala, 696 e-books & 3800 audios available, 15 Urdu textbooks converted in Unicode font for specially-abled learners, 367 text book created & 14,442 free e-contents available. SWAYAM PRABHA TV Channel (32) devoted to telecast of high-quality educational programmes launched with 24x7 telecast. It provides one earmarked TV channel per class from 1 to 12.

(v) **Reduction in Social and Extra-curricular Activities:** Extra-curricular, athletic, or community activities as a measure of reducing physical contact have been cancelled. This has been rolled out regionally and nationally by governments looking to enforce social distancing.

(vi) **Preventive Actions:** Most governments have undertaken awareness campaigns through schools on hygiene and sanitation to students. In addition, primary schools must organize contact teaching for those grades 1-3 students whose parents work in critical positions such as health, education, logistics, supermarkets etc.

(vi) **Technology Driven Education with Equity:** The initiative include Manodarpan-Psychosocial support initiative for students, teachers and families for mental health and emotional well-being to be launched immediately; New National Curriculum and Pedagogical framework for school, early childhood and teachers integrated with global and 21st century skill requirements and National Foundational Literacy and Numeracy Mission to be launched by December, 2020 to ensure that every child attains learning level and outcomes in Grade 5 by 2025.

(vii) **Technology Driven Online Education:** The package announced by Prime Minister of India envisaged online education at the grassroots level with DTH operators like Tata Sky & Airtel to Air educational video content to enhance the reach of these channels; Coordination with States of India to share air time (4hrs daily) on the SWAYAM PRABHA channel to telecast their education related content; DIKSHA platform has had 61 crore hits from 24th March to 17th May, 2020 and 200 new textbooks added to e-Paathshaala.

Suggestions

The paradigm shift necessitates innovation in capacity development endeavours with the need for new methods of education delivery in teaching profession. Following measures may be taken to improve the condition of rural education amidst COVID-19:

(i) **Use of education resources:** In environment of low capacity and weak infrastructure, some states have used education facilities and staff to support the larger community during the crisis. In these cases, attention is needed to define a clear path to returning the schools to their initial purpose once the crisis is over.

(ii) **Assessment of Impact to Draw Future Lessons:** Meanwhile, the estimation may be undertaken to assess the disruptions impact on learning – such as school closures, students and teachers' absenteeism, exams delays, families without sufficient means to send their children back to school to draw lessons for future to handle such situations.

(iii) **Communication Campaigns and Information Sharing:** The situation demandsto assure parents of the safety of their children returning to schools as communities have been ravaged by disaster and there is distrust in Government efforts to undertake measures. Communication could include a timeline of school sanitization, dissemination of screening protocols, provision of hand washing stations etc. accessible for all and supplies.

(iv) **Resilient Reopening of Schools:** Bringing education facilities back to the original condition may not be enough if wash stations, availability of water and soaps in schoolsor toilets are not available and leaves students vulnerable again to future health risks.

SAMARTH: Systemic Reforms to Improve Quality of Education in Himachal Pradesh

State Government initiated state-wide systemic reforms to improve the quality of education in the state's 14000 elementary government schools. The focus of the programme "Samarth" is to improve the learning levels of students through *systemic interventions*. The key focus of the programme is to *Improve learning levels by 8-10 percentage points, Achieve grade-level competencies for at least 75% students across elementary grades and Ensure Himachal is among top 3 states in National Achievement Survey (NAS)*. The programme has been divided into three phases: diagnostic, design and implementation.

- *During the diagnostic phase a full-scale problem identification exercise was conducted wherein each of the 12 districts in Himachal were visited, large scale surveys were carried out, and expert interviews and discussions were held with various internal and external stakeholders.*
- *During the design phase, best practices from other states were studied and solutions were designed to specifically address identified problems within Himachal's unique culture and context.*
- *The programme is currently in the implementation phase with multiple initiatives on the ground.*

Besides this, the Government of Himachal Pradesh in lockdown phase has started Har Ghar Pathshala, a whatsapp based education system with easy learning material for class 1-12 where the easy learning material has been prepared and webhosted date-wise. The same material and worksheets are supplied in the whatsapp groups for children for different subjects.

(v) **Support to Family Income:** The crisis might impact attendance due to the economic impacts in particular where the children who have subsumed into farming and other works. In case, the assessment identifies such instances, states could consider some incentives to bring the children back to schools.

(vi) **Collaboration with Private Sector:** To explore the possibility with private sector service providers to provide content already developed is a useful option to explore. A key element in the discussion of using smartphones is establishing partnerships with telecom providers to allow for zero charges for content downloaded from the Ministry of Education or any agency that hosts learning resources platforms. TV, which can use captions to support various language learners and students with disabilities or sign language interpreters to reach deaf learners, and radio options can be used for lower grades.

Combining Technology with Community Engagement in Odisha

ThinkZone, an NGO, leveraged existing resources- anganwadi workers and community educators. It trained them to deliver quality early-grade education programs by using ThinkZone's technology, teaching resources, classroom activities, and management tools. Keeping in mind the lack of reliable internet connectivity in rural India, ThinkZone school-in-a-box solution included a mobile application with access to offline educational material. These lesson plans were further aided by charts, maps, and other lesson material included in the proprietary box. Its Early Childhood Education Program aimed at building the physical, emotional, social, linguistic and cognitive skills of children aged 3-6 years. Its Primary Grade Education Program adopted an evidence-based 'Teaching-at-the-Right-Level' approach. Children are not taught based on their age but on their skill-level. The focus is on developing their language (reading, writing, comprehension) and basic arithmetic skills.

As COVID-19 hit India, aanganwadis and government schools went into lockdown. However, ThinkZone team had been developing a home-based model of learning for parents to engage their children. In this model, low-income group families can call to a number and learn about quality learning modules which they can use to teach their children. Apart from that, the model also has the facility for the parent to receive bi-weekly IVR-based calls and SMSs on their mobile phones regarding DIY learning modules. The user-friendly modules can be understood and delivered by the parent regardless of their literacy level or type of mobile phone. Parents can also schedule these automated calls for ease.

Conclusion

It is a known fact that the educational institutions are most vulnerable for the spread of the disease due to the mass gathering in the classrooms. Therefore unless, the infection is totally eradicated, it is difficult to bring back the students to the schools, colleges, universities and other educational institutions. Resuming normal classes in classrooms, therefore, seems a distant dream at this time. The school education institutions will have to reflect internally, with the participation of students and teachers, about the lessons learned during the crisis about the teaching and learning processes. The acquired experience to be capitalized for a redesign of processes, maximizing the advantages of face-to-face classes while making the most of technologies. The policy makers for rural education will haveto develop innovation and pedagogical support for developing the pedagogical competences of teachers, to promote pedagogical innovation and accumulate and disseminate the findings resulting from their evaluation. It further needs to undertake the path of a necessary pedagogical renewal that favours both quality and equality.

References

Alvi, Muzna & Gupta Manavi. (2020) *Learning in times of lockdown: how COVID-19 is affecting education and food security in India*, Food Security volume 12, pages 793–796.

Burgess, Simon and Sievertsen, Hans Henrik. (2020) *Schools, skills, and learning: The impact of COVID-19 on education,* VoxEu.org, Research-based policy analysis and commentary from leading economists, Web hosted on :https://voxeu.org/article/impact-COVID-19-education

Department of Elementary Education, Himachal Pradesh, (2020). https://himachal.nic.in/index1.php?lang=1&dpt_id=16&level=0&linkid=4066&lid=13229

Gharde, Dr.Yachna Ramesh. (2019) Growth Of Education In Rural India : A Contemporary Study, Youth Incorporated, https://youthincmag.com/growth-of-education-in-rural-india-a-contemporary-study

Gupta Shivani, (2020), *Education on hold: Amid the COVID lockdown, children in rural India will suffer the most,* Gaon Connection, https://en.gaonconnection.com/education-on-hold-the-impact-will-be-seen-in-children-in-poor-and-low-resource-settings-in-rural-areas/

Kaur, Ramandeep. (2019) Rural Education in India, Education Blog/India https://www.mapsofindia.com/my-india/education/india-needs-education-especially-rural-education

Kumari, Anshu and Maithreyi, R. (26th May, 2020), *Covid 19 and the Interruption to Schooling in Rural Karnataka,* Critical Childhoods and Youth Studies Collective webhosted on www.khpt.org

Planning Department, *Himachal Pradesh. (2019) Drishti Himachal Pradesh-2030, Sustainable Development Goals*, Planning Department, Government of Himachal Pradesh, Shimla and National Foundation for India, New Delhi.

UDISE Report, (2019) Department of School Education & Literacy, Ministry of Education, Government of India http://udiseplus.gov.in/

informationDetails.action;jsessionid=0181258061BDDF5159B38A9CD9A44871?fileId=4

UNESCO. (2020).*COVID-19 and Higher Education: Today and Tomorrow, Impact analysis, policy responses and recommendations.* UNESCO International Institute for Higher Education in Latin America and the Caribbean

United Nations, (AUGUST 2020).*Policy Brief: Education during COVID-19 and beyond.* Web hosted on :https://www.un.org/development/desa/dspd/wp-content/uploads/sites/22/2020/08/sg_policy_brief_COVID-19_and_education_august_2020.pdf..................

World Health Organisation, (2020) https://www.who.int/teams/health-workforce/about

COVID-19-lockdown-impact-global-pandemic-on-education-sector/https://www.indiatoday.in/education-today/featurephilia/story/-1698391-2020-07-08

Growth-of-education-in-rural-india-a-contemporary-study/https://youthincmag.com/

COVID-19-crisis-sheds-light-on-the-need-for-a-new-education-model.htmlhttps://educationtimes.com/article/editors-pick/75096945

Chapter - 14

Impact of COVID-19 on Rural Society of Sikkim

— Ms. Jashi M. Gurung

Introduction

Covid-19 Pandemic is known as a systematic crisis which has affected economies and societies along with health emergency in an incomparable way. (Hall, Nayyar, Kumar et.al, 2020). As per WHO reports, the health system faced a great challenge due to the lack of therapeutics or vaccines to treat or stop COVID-19. However, the study has revealed COVID-19 has created a situation similar to Spanish flu (1918) and Bombay Plague (1896) which has increased the worldwide crude mortality rate. The WHO has made an important protocol for COVID-19 which is applicable worldwide. Among many rules of COVID-19, a 'social distancing' is an important rule which entails practicing at least one- meter distance in any meeting spots. As per the United Nations Educational, Scientific and Cultural Organisation (UNESCO) report 2020, to decrease and stop the spread of viruses the restaurants, movie theatres, gymnasiums, clubs, universities, schools, canteens, shopping malls, etc., are all locked down over the world. Only a few important government offices, medical stores, grocery shops were allowed to open at certain regulated periods with least man powers. Many studies of COVID-19 revealed the vulnerability caused by it to the employees of informal sectors including migrant labourers and marginal sections, the surge of domestic violence in the family etc.,

All Indian states and Union territories have also been infected. The highest infected state includes Maharashtra, Tamil Nadu, Andhra Pradesh, Karnataka, Kerala, Delhi, Mumbai, Bihar, etc., where the virus has caused severe challenges which resulted into lethal Pandemic. Lakhs of the population have affected and died in India due to clusters of cases transmission of COVID-19. The disease has created a disorder into the economic, health, political, psychological, and social sectors of India. (Singh, 2020), (Haleem, 2020).

Effects of COVID-19 in Sikkim

Sikkim is a rural and developing State of India consisting of the 6.1-lakh (Census 2011) population. The government has initiated a different effective measure to save the people and State from the Novel virus. Such as Sikkim's Health and Family Welfare Department has taken an early precautionary measure since January 2020 which has also been announced into the gram panchayat levels. Screening facilities were also employed in the Rangpo check post for every traveller. Isolation ward and quarantine centers are initiated in the different districts of the state. Restriction of the entry of foreign nationals, all government, and private schools, colleges, training institutes are closed till the normalization. Distribution of rations is also initiated by the government to the migrant labourers, Below Poverty Level family, and others who do not possess state documents. Section 144 of the IPC enforced to reduce public gathering and ensure social distancing. The Rapid Antigen tests are also conducting in and around the containment zone to detect the symptomatic and asymptomatic COVID-19 patients and further to reduce the transmission.

The case of COVID-19 in Sikkim was first detected on 23rd May 2020 who had travelled history of Delhi. Nevertheless, continuously the cases of COVID-19 have increased in the State. Till the third week of August 2020, the virus has spiked more than 1400.

Table 1: COVID-19 Case in Sikkim

Number of COVID-19 cases	*Frequency*	*Percentage %*
Active	418	28.25 %
Recovered	1054	71.31 %
Deceased	3	0.2 %
Total confirmed	1478	100%

Till dated 26th August 2020, 71.31% of infected patients are fully cured and discharged and the remaining 28.25% are under the treatment in different medical quarantine and isolation ward of Sikkim. Despite the continuous effort from the medical team to cure the infected persons, unfortunately, Sikkim recorded the first COVID-19 death case of a 72 years man on 27th July 2020. Till now it records three deaths which constituted of 0.2%. Source: Arogya Setu [Accessed on 26thAugust 2020]

Lockdown and social distancing as a major step have been initiated and implemented from the third week of March to the end of May 2020 to control the transmission of the disease. However, due to the alarming increase of the virus, the State has extended the lockdown till 31st August 2020 with few permitted vehicles, stores, and a few important offices to be functional. However, the cases have spread and increased in different parts of Sikkim including Chanatar, Rongli, Central Pendam, Duga, Zitlang, Timburbung, Ranipool, Singtam, Burtuk, Namchi, Sumerdung, Deorali etc., Many Gram Panchayat Units of East, West, and South districts are sealed as containment and red zones by the state. The cluster transmission outbreak in the different areas of Sikkim has created havoc because of the new cases.

Objectives and Methodology

Main objectives of this study are to understand the effect of COVID-19 in Sikkim and to examine the different socio-economic challenge by COVID-19 in a rural society of Sikkim. This study is qualitative. For this study purpose, both primary and secondary sources were used. A semi-structured interview schedule has been used to have an in-depth data collection of the subject matter. Purposive sampling has been used to select the 40respondents from the containment zone area of Chanatar and Central Pendam GPU of Sikkim.The data is collected through the telephonic interviews. The secondary sources like government official reports, articles, social sites, journals on COVID-19 are also reviewed for relevant data. Observation method is also employed to understand the present situation in Sikkim. This study began from the 15th of July to 16th August 2020. Therefore, the study is only limited to two objectives.

Profile of Respondents

Table 2.1: Total number of Respondents

Gender	*Frequency*	*Percent*	*Cumulative Percent*
WOMEN	20	50.0	50.0
MEN	20	50.0	100.0
Total	40	100.0	

The total number of respondents (*n*) = 40in which 50% men and 50% women are interviewed.

Table 2.2: Category wise number of Respondents

CATEGORY	*Frequency*	*Percent*	*Cumulative Percent*
MBC	5	12.5	12.5
OBC	13	32.5	45.0
SC	8	20.0	65.0
ST	14	35.0	100.0
Total	40	100.0	

Table 2.2 represents total category of respondents constituted of 100%. In which 12.5% are Most Backward Caste, 32.5% are Other Backward Caste, 20% are Scheduled Caste and 35% are Scheduled Tribes.Table 2.3: Religion of the Respondents.

RELIGION	*Frequency*	*Percent*	*Cumulative Percent*
BUDDHIST	12	30.0	30.0
CHRISTIAN	5	12.5	42.5
HINDU	23	57.5	100.0
Total	40	100.0	

Table 2.3 shows the religious group of the respondents out of which 30% are Buddhists, 12.5 % are christians and 57.5% Hindus.Table 2.4:Type of Family of the Respondents

Types of Family	*Frequency*	*Percent*	*Cumulative Percent*
JOINT	10	25.0	25.0
NUCLEAR	30	75.0	100.0
Total	40	100.0	

Table 2.4 represents total number of family type in which joint families included 25% and 75% are nuclear families.

Table 2.5: Occupation of the Respondents

Occupation	*Frequency*	*Percent*	*Cumulative Percent*
BUSINESS	3	7.5	7.5
CASUAL WORKER	4	10.0	17.5
CONTRACT WORKER	3	7.5	25.0
DRIVER	1	2.5	27.5
FARMER	3	7.5	35.0
GOVT.JOB	7	17.5	52.5
LIQUIOR COMPANY	8	20.0	72.5
PHARMA COMPANY	10	25.0	97.5
PVT.TEACHER	1	2.5	100.0
Total	40	100.0	

Table 2.5 included the types of occupation of the respondentsin which25% families are dependent on the pharmaceutical companies and 20% in liquor companies, 17.5% are government employees, 7.5% contract worker, 7.5% depends on business, 10%are causal workers, 2.5% driver, 2.5% is Pvt.Teacher.

Findings and Analysis: *Impact of COVID-19 on Rural Society*

As we all live in a society in which one has to have an 'interaction' and 'interdependent' with each other regularly to survive. One individual is not self-sufficient. Society is a network of inter-relationship (Maclver and Page,1950) in which the economic, educational, health, and social aspects of a particular society are equally interrelated with one another depending upon each other for a function of the whole. If one part of the society is disrupted it affects the other parts also which also leads to the pathological stage (Parson,1956). As per the United Nations Department of Economic and Social Affairs (UN DESA) COVID-19 is 'attacking the societies at the core'. Meanings the disease has been affecting to the everyday basics of family including access to food, job, educations, medical checkups, transportation, communication etc., and Unquestionably, the COVID-19 has affected the lives of people in many aspects which is yet to be studied completely. Nevertheless, being 'isolated' from a normal routine for more than weeks, months have created a different social challenge in their everyday lives.

(i) **Division between the Haves and Haves Not-** On a macro level, the State economy standard has been dropped down. Each source of income has declined by COVID-19. Tourism is one of the main sources of economy in Sikkim which runs multiple hotels, homestays, catering services, restaurants, travel agencies, etc.,isgreatly affected by it (Bhutia, Sherpa, 2020). Apart from tourism,agricultural practices and small-scale business, different private pharmaceutical companies, are also being affected by the COVID-19 where more than thousands of youth are currently enrolled and are dependent on for their survival. The different companies including Alkem Laboratory, Sun pharma plant - II, Microlab, Torrent, Sikkim distilleries, etc., has become containment zone. Therefore, the pharmaceutical employees are under the responsibilityand worrisome situations to continue their work.

Similarly, at micro-level many farmers, taxi drivers, carpenters, construction workers, temporary employees,etc., are also under the financial crises to manage their daily activities and the necessities. The study found families who do not have a regular source of income and does not hold any savings including private employees, manual labors, farmers,taxi drivers, causal workersare facing great problem during the Pandemic.With the effect of the economic base, the other everyday livelihoods have also been affected.Including the payment of school fees, loans, rented rooms, and leased hotels to outdoor daily activites. Being declared as containment zone, there is restriction in the movement of people and taxis in and round the red zones. Due to which the organic and freshvegetables that was available and sold in informal or local market are rare. Simultaneously, the local vegetable prices have also increased in which poor people have lacked to consume a nutritious diet despite knowing to keep up a healthy dietary routine.

> Miss Darjee says,"*I am thankful for having every facility in my home during this crisis because my family has a reliable government job under holding a stable income, my family did not have to face the situation where I would need to think, what should I eat tomorrow? If I have money, I can manage to bring every essential even in a year of lockdown as online delivery are also there. But other peoples are suffering".*
>
> *A narrative made by a woman aged around 55yrs, - "Mukhiya ko Ghar ma makai, Hami bhokkai". (Rich people have plates of food but we are empty stomach).*
>
> A brief narrative of a pharmaceutical employee, - "*During this COVID-19 situation, I wish to stay safe at home with family. I have a 6 years old daughter and wife at home. If someway I get infected, my family will also get infected. We adults can handle it but I cannot see my daughter being suffering. I will not get a full salary if I remain absent on working days. However, I am not allowed to remain home even if I wish to because I may be terminated from my job. Therefore, to be safe and continuously go for duty, I'm taking Immunity dose in the hope of not getting contacted by the virus".*

The above narrative is of one employee and a woman. However, it's a fact of hundreds of employees and manual workers in Sikkim in this pandemic. COVID-19 has explicitly created the economic inequalities between the haves and haves not in rural society of Sikkim.

(ii) **Educational Barrier among the Parents, Children (Students) and Teachers-** School is an institution that plays an important role in the overall development of children from a basic skill to a creative idea. Durkheim and Parson outlined that school is the second institution after family where socialization takes place and the school acts as a bridge between the family and society as a whole that prepares children for an adult role (Haralambous, 2016). During the school days, children spend 6-7 hours in the schools and they learn many new things through the institution's rules and values, books, interactions with classmates and teachers, by outdoor games, etc., However, due to the closures of schools in this pandemic new online teaching and learning techniques has been initiated by every institution including government, private schools, colleges, and universities. It's been six-months educational institutes are completely closed. All syllabus, homework, exams, presentations, and sessional tests are communicated through online sources. WhatsApp, Facebook, and Google meet are widely practiced to impart education.

This study found the responsibilities of the parents on their children have increased in this pandemic while protecting and maintaining their children's safety every time and helping them to prepare for tests. In a family where there are more than two siblingswho are students shared the same gadgets or seek help from the kins member to access phones and the internet to complete their work on time.

Nevertheless, being at the peak rainy season there occurs frequent electric cuts due to the natural calamities. The children (students) and teachers were not able to continue their online classes due to the interrupted internet connectivity of jio, Vodafone, and Airtel network in the villages. However, in many instances, parents were untrained to teach the school syllabus and help in their children's studies.

(iii) **Social Stigma and Alienation Due to COVID-19-** Social stigma has been defined as an act when members of particular group labels or treats humans as 'other'. It also separates 'us' from 'them' (Link & Phelan, 2001). The United Nation reports show social stigma and discrimination has increased associated with an infected person along with their families. Even in Indian society, the stigmatization has been faced by infected persons, containment zone's people along with families and groups. Social rejection has become intensive in terms of availing basic needs from accessing housing, accessing health check-ups, buying food, and employment.

Health system of the entire nation has been under challengeable situation due to the inadequate infrastructures and medical solutions to control COVID-19 which resulted into lakhs of deaths. Therefore, in this pandemic, there has been a high load and responsibilities on the prevailing medical system where the health professional and the front-line warrior worked and still working staking their life at risk. (Sherin, 2020), (Haleem, 2020), et.al Many studies have outlined the loss of medical worker's lives while treating the patients. Sikkim being a small state also has a limited medical resource. There is a limited number of medical infrastructures, limited doctors, and staff in state hospitals. Therefore, in the present situation different institutes, resorts and hostels are converted into provisional COVID-19 care centers by the State where the positive patients are kept for the treatment. Despite of inadequate health facilities the existing health system, and government are in constant effort to save the patients from the disease.

However, this study found that the family members who fall sick during the lockdown faced a severe challenge while seeking a medical checkup in time. Firstly, there was a restriction in the movement of the daily taxi services. Due to which they had to reserved taxis to go for nearby Primary Health Centre. Secondly, in the visited PHCs there was unavailability of required medicinal facilities and family members and patients were referred to visit district hospitals. Meanwhile they were represented indifferently because of belonging from in and around the COVID-19 containment zone areas.

On the other hand, study also found the villagers have lacked social solidarity among the neighbours who were helpful earlier. More than the disease of COVID -19, the social disease that has been created by people in the society has obstructed the people's relationship with each other. The environment has been created as of fear and stress by the COVID-19's unofficial and false News, sometimes uncaring acts towards infected families, and containment zone peoples.

Conclusion

COVID-19 a pandemic disease has created a situation which one never would have imagined in 2020. It has risked and threatened the global economy, educational, health, psychological, and social lives of people causing millions of deaths worldwide. It has also affected the Sikkim and its society in different aspects. Despite many challenges in Sikkim, the government, NGOs, frontline workers, and people are still in the process to prevent the COVID-19 for further transmissions. The state as a whole is in a long wait to revive its loss in terms of economy and social relationships.

During this difficult phase, the government, panchayats, non-governmental organizations, and local youths are ensuring various assistance either by providing rations, incentives, and medical support. The biological disorder caused by COVID-19 can be curable at a particular level but the social disease of fear, anxiety, alienation, etc., caused by it is incurable to many extents if there prevail unconstructive social relationships among the individuals in a society.

Therefore, to fight this Pandemic along with government officials, health workers, police, media, etc., each needs to act responsibly. Fear and complete lockdown may not be the ultimate solution for smooth running and reviving a normal situation. Everyone has a responsibility to fulfill it, one has to moved out because people have a fear to suffer from starvation more than the disease. Yet, no scientific studies have predicted when the COVID-19 will dissolve completely. Nevertheless, it might take time to test and implement the vaccine in different parts of the world. Therefore, community education about the risk factor, socio-economic problems, necessary remedies to tackle the situation, and a hopeful, motivating knowledge and practical help can be imparted into the masses through any means of communication or social media.

References

Assembly, T. G. (2020). *RACIAL DISCRIMINATION IN THE CONTEXT OF THE COVID-19 CRISIS 1. What is the impact of COVID-19 on the health of people of African descent, people of Asian descent, Roma, and other marginalized groups? Some recommended actions:* (June), 1–12.

Bhutia, P. C. (2020). *Effect of Covid-19 on Sikkim tourism -a Case Study Tathapi Effect of Covid-19 on Sikkim tourism – a Case Study*. (June).

Bhutia, S. (2020). Novel Coronavirus Disease 2019 (Covid-19): Strategies and Statistics of Sikkim State-India Up To 1/04/2020. *Indian Research Journal of Pharmacy and Science*, 7(1), 2095–2100. https://doi.org/10.21276/irjps.2020.7.1.7

Combating COVID-19 Pandemic in Sikkim A Report. Sikkim State Disaster Management Authority (SSDMA) Land Revenue & Disaster Management Department April-2020. http://www.ssdma.nic.in/Uploads/PdfFiles/interim%20report%20covid-19%20Issue-1.pdf [Accessed on 6 August 2020].

Government of Sikkim official website, [Online], Available; https://sikkim.gov.in [Accessed on 8 August 2020].

Haleem, A., Javaid, M., & Vaishya, R. (2020). Current Medicine Research and Practice Effects of COVID-19 pandemic in daily life. *Current Medicine Research and Practice*, (April), 10 12. https://doi.org/10.1016/j.cmrp.2020.03.011.

Haralambous, M. (1980) Sociological Themes and Perspectives; Oxford University Press.

Hall, J., Jahic, A., Nayyar, S., Ortubia, A., Rivera, C., Tapia, H., … Slay, B. (2020). *2020 HUMAN DEVELOPMENT PERSPECTIVES COVID-19 AND HUMAN DEVELOPMENT: Assessing the Crisis, Envisioning the Recovery The team that created this report includes Pedro*.

Haralambous, M., & Heald, R. M. (2013). SOCIOLOGY: Themes and Perspectives. New Delhi: Oxford University Press.

Mills, C. W. (1959) Sociological Imagination; Oxford University Press.

Kumar, S. U., Kumar, D. T., & Christopher, B. P. (2020). *The Rise and Impact of COVID-19 in India*. *7*(May), 1–7. https://doi.org/10.3389/fmed.2020.00250.

Sherin, a. (2020). *Coronavirus disease 2019 (COVID-19): a challenge of protecting the general population and health-care workers 2019* (April),2019–2021. https://doi.org/10.35845/kmuj.2020.20224

Singh, J. (2020). *COVID - 19's Impact on the Society*. *19*(April).

Sikkim chronicle official website, [Online], Available; www.sikkimchronicle.com [Accessed on 9 August 2020].

UnitedNationofficialwebsite,[Online],Available;https://www.un.org/development/desa/dspd/2020/04/ social-impact-of-covid-19 [Accessed on 10 August 2020].

Chapter - 15

MGNREGA and Social Audit amidst COVID-19

— Dr. Vikas Jha

COVID-19 and MGNREGA

Lockdown in April-May, 2020 due to COVID-19 led to mass migration of workers from cities to villages. Despite strict measures by the government to stop any movement, people facing lost jobs and high cost of living in the cities began to walk back or use whatever transportation was available to travel to their home villages. After starting Shramik Express trains, the migration increased many fold, and all state governments started preparing to provide livelihoods for villagers returning home. The central and state governments started transferring funds to Gram Panchayats so that the Mahatma Gandhi National Rural Employment Guarantee Act (MGNREGA) could be launched immediately.

Bihar and Uttar Pradesh witnessed the maximum amount of interstate migration (per data of state government) in the period April–June 2020. About 28 lakhs migrants[1] have returned to Bihar and 32 lakhs migrants[2] returned to Uttar Pradesh (UP). Hence it would be appropriate to discuss and analyze data of expenses incurred and job creation through MGNREGA in these states[3]. As Rs. 1,01,500 crores have been allocated in the MGNREGA for 2020–21, it will be pertinent to see if how public accountability mechanisms, such as social audits, are working in these states[4].

UP and Bihar started preparing for providing work through MGNREGA to migrants as they began arriving in their native places in May–June 2020. The UP government started work under natural resources management, such as deepening of ponds and rejuvenation works, in nearly twenty-two rivers in a big way under MGNREGA[5]. An analysis of workwise category of estimated costs in UP during April–June 2020 showed that 75 percent of MGNREGA funds were allocated for natural resources management (water conservation, irrigation, and water bodies) and 20 percent of funds were used for development of individual assets for vulnerable sections[6]. A similar analysis for Bihar showed that 83 percent of MGNREGA[7] funds were allocated for natural resources management, specially flood management[8], and 12 percent of funds were used for development of individual assets for vulnerable sections.This demonstrates that work prioritization has been quite appropriate and relevant to the needs of the community in the two states.

Table 1: Patter of Work Demand in Bihar and Uttar Pradesh

Bihar: Work demand pattern comparison of FY 2019-2020 & FY 2020-21				
	2019	***Persons who worked***	***2020***	***Persons who worked***
1.	April 2019	13,08,554	April 2020	9,30,695
2.	May 2019	14,54,517	May 2020	23,19,766
3.	June 2019	15,36,069	June 2020	29,07,349
Uttar Pradesh: Work demand pattern comparison of FY 2019-2020 & FY 2020-21				
	2019	***Persons who worked***	***2020***	***Persons who worked***
1.	April 2019	13,28,208	April 2020	12,76,189
2.	May 2019	15,91,391	May 2020	65,69,487
3.	June 2019	26,37,473	June 2020	92,54,574

Source: nrega.nic.in

The next important question is whether MGNREGA has been able to provide employment to huge number of migrants in both states.The work-demand pattern for Bihar shows that 8.65 lakhs more people worked in May 2020 than in May 2019; while in UP, a whopping 49.78 lakhs more persons worked in May 2020 than in May 2019. For June 2020, theincrease in persons who worked was 13.71 lakhs in Bihar and 70 lakhs in UP. The employment of nearly 10 million people in water works in the two states will certainly g boost water conservation efforts which will yield good result in future. The scheme is no doubt providing employment to migrants who had shifted in huge numbers to these two states.

Social Audit of MGNREGA amidst COVID-19

The expenditure in MGNREGA work for the period April 2020 – June 2020 has been Rs. 1,692 crores for Bihar and Rs. 3773 crores for Uttar Pradesh[9], testifying that government prioritization for MGNREGA works. However, the actual number of people working and being paid and the quality of assets being created can only be verified by government department audits and social audits. While the ministry of Panchayati Raj Government of India has created an application, Audit Online, of the scheme to ensure accountability in utilization of funds in Gram Panchayat[10]. But the social audit process required support and guidance in Gram Panchayats. Though the directorate of Social Audit, UP, has issued a format[11] for social audit, how this process should be carried out in present challenging times needs clarity.

Table 2: Social Audit in Bihar

Bihar: Social Audit Verification data FY 2019-20					
Total GPs	***Total no of GPs audited once***	***Expenditure***	***Amt audited***	***Total Works***	***Total verified***
8530	2647	1185 cr	492 cr	4,32,144	1,14,561
Bihar: Social Audit Verification data FY 2020-21					
Total GPs	***Total no of GPs audited once***	***Expenditure***	***Amt audited***	***Total Works***	***Total verified***
8530	0	0	0	0	0

Source: nrega.nic.in.

Table 3: Social Audit in Uttar Pradesh

Uttar Pradesh: Social Audit Verification data FY 2019-20					
Total GPs	***Total no of GPs audited once***	***Expenditure***	***Amt audited***	***Total Works***	***Total verified***
58906	46497	4091cr	2984cr	14,43,154	6,61,484
Uttar Pradesh: Social Audit Verification data FY 2020-21					
Total GPs	***Total no of GPs audited once***	***Expenditure***	***Amt audited***	***Total Works***	***Total verified***
58906	5	53,83,076	51,38,439	178	24

Source: nrega.nic.in

In the year 2020-21, table 3 shows that only five of 58,906 Gram Panchayats in Uttar Pradesh have been able to conduct social audits, and only 13 percent of the works have been verified. Thus Gram Panchayats are facing tremendous difficulties in conducting social audits in the current financial year. Table 2 shows that no Gram Panchayat, out of 8,530 Gram Panchayats, has been able to facilitate a social audit in the FY 2020–21 in Bihar.

While in the year 2019-20, 80 percent of Gram Panchayats participated in the social audit and 49 percent of total works were verified in Uttar Pradesh (table 3). Similarly, in Bihar, 31 percent of Gram Panchayats participated in the social audit and 26 percent of total works were verified in financial year 2019-20 (table 2). It demonstrates that social audit process requires lot of strengthening in the Gram Panchayats. NREGA guidelines on social audit and CAG social audit standards have not been implemented in the Gram Panchayats on mass scale. Social audit unit or society in the states have not been able to give social audit the shape of movement and mainstream social audit exercise into functioning of Gram Panchayats and gram sabhas. Hence social audit process is carried out mostly organized without participation of people.

Even where it is organized, the discussion centers on redress of individual grievances not on overall functioning and asset verification of the programs. A social audit of key government programs in Pahsarapurvi panchayat, Begusarai in December, 2019 shows that people mainly raised issue of non-payment of subsidy of toilets which shows people do not have information or capacity to carry out asset verification and identify financial irregularities in government programs[12]. Even where the issues are raised by people as it was done in social audit of NREGA in Jamua panchayat Araria district, Bihar, villagers who raised the issues were open threatened and beaten up and police had to be called to give protection to villagers[13]. It makes one wonder whether online raising of issues can be safer medium where a group of villagers together post the photos or list of issues on the social audit unit's portals. The uploads will be official records which can be monitored rural development departments at state and national level.

New ways of conducting social audit should be explored in current times which can be relevant social economic context of Bihar and Uttar Pradesh and in COVID times as well when restrictions on gathering and movement is there.

Interesting CAG social audit standards has clearly laid out framework which is relevant for all times including natural disasters and pandemic. Outlining the objectives, it emphasizes on educating and informing people, promote people participation in implementation, provide collective platform to express their needs and grievances and improve capacity of all stakeholders[14]. The social audit standards elaborating in minimum principles of transparency and accountability, it focuses on display and dissemination of information, and multimedia communications. It says "all relevant information regarding programmes and public institutions should be proactively displayed in different modes and medium ensuring local language compatibility"[15]. The different modes and medium can be video recording and uploading of documents on government web sites. Similarly, panchayats can also disseminate key information of NREGA on what app groups of villagers.

Further, the standards point out that multimedia communications can result in sharing and free flow of information without any hindrance. Hence new and emerging technologies especially social media and online platforms should be effectively used in social audit[16]. These principles have gain more relevance amidst COVID-19.

Suggestions

It is time to work out appropriate mechanisms for social audits in the new scenario, so that huge amounts of money and work do not go unverified by people. Gram Sabha and Jun Sunwais may not be feasible for at least a year due to restriction of COVID-19. The possible mechanisms for social audits can be online and offline tools with the option of uploading on the portal of department of rural development of the state government. The availability of smart phones and network connectivity will be an issue in some areas, but forming social audit teams consisting of youth, especially migrants from cities, community leaders, and Self Help groups can be the starting point for social audit exercise.The resource person of the social audit unit of the states will be key link to coordinate between members of Gram Panchayats and the social audit team. The social audit team can record the information related to social audit offline and upload them when they are in connectivity zone. It is important to consider some options for carrying out the social audit in these challenging times.

1. **Transparency in sharing MGNREGA details[17]**: All important information related to the scheme must be exhibited in common places in the Gram Panchayat. Some community leaders, youth groups, and SHG should check its compliance by Gram Panchayats and report any noncompliances in the recording during the social audit. The government of India has plans to connect all six lakhs villages of India by internet in 1000 days[18], it will also give internet accessibility to villagers as broadband connection goes into the villages. It may solve internet connectivity issues in the villages. The villagers can thus check information related to development expenditure in the village in Gram Panchayat Bhawan or common service center or mobiles.

2. **Physical verification of assets**: Social audit team with guidance from the resource person can carry out physical verifications of assets after intimating Gram Panchayats. They should click photos, make videos, and upload them on the government portal. If vested interest create obstacle or physically threaten the social audit team then photos or recordings of such incidences should also be uploaded by the villagers.
3. **Review and documentary analysis**: The social audit teamcan review the documents of MGNREGA, namely income, expenditure, muster rolls, and payments, to analyze if the money can be spent forthe right purposes. They can record the group's opinions and post on the website of social audit society/unit.
4. **Opinions of SHGs and women-elected representatives**: Voices of women-elected representatives and SHGs members should have separate space, and they should record their opinions on the issues, such as the number of women getting employment, regular payment, and needs of women being addressed by asset creation in the villages. Enterprising women SHG members have mobile phone and as operate their small business on mobile, these women can be the leaders in the social audit exercise in their Gram Panchayats.
5. **Video recording and uploading of ward-level meetings**: Social audit teams,especially youth groups, community leaders, and SHGs, can mobilize villagers for attending ward-level small meetings with social distancing in the areas from where large numbers of workers work for the MGNREGA. In these meeting, the findings of social audit team should be shared. The sarpanchand other panchayat functionaries should facilitate the exercise. Sarpanch will share the details of expenditures, money received, and workers employed on the sites. Oral evidences of villagers on the number of assets created, quality of assets, and issues related to employment and payment can be recorded and uploaded on the platform created by the social audit society/unit of the state. Efforts should be made to cover four wards in a day, so that 25 percent of the village population is covered.

Conclusion

The critical question is the cooperation of the sarpanch in the social audit being led by a newly constituted social audit team. The resistance of the sarpanch to entry of new groups, viz. youth and SHGs, can be addressed with the appropriate guidelines of social audit society/unit in each state. The presence of resource persons of social audit society during social audit can neutralize the vested interests in Gram Panchayat as s/he can report the issue to the society. Social audit society should also issue instructions/orders on how social audit processes should be carried in the Gram Panchayat in context of constraints on public gatherings due to COVID-19.

The villagers and SHGs can be proactive and take necessary steps for conducting social audit using new social media tools but key question is will social audit unit / society of the states match steps with villagers. Can the social audit units or rural development department provide platforms to villagers for uploading social audit photos, films and documents? Further, can the system of monitoring and tracking in the units be robust and actions are initiated within a certain time frame? The lack of such system may demotivate the villagers and use of new technologies may run out of steam.

Hence, the social audit society of the state government should refurbish their websites and create platforms for social audits in the new context. At present, these websites are in very nascent stage. The society should collate and compile the data of social audits of the Gram Panchayats and forward them to the Department of Rural development. All these efforts can pave the way for better utilization of MGNREGA funds, build the capacity of villagers to use online platforms, and deter vested interests from appropriating the funds.

References

1. Seehttps://www.livehindustan.com/bihar/story-bihar-govt-in-supreme-court-28-lakh-migrant-have-return-to-state-we-are-taking-all-steps-for-providing-them-employment-3260834.html.
2. Seehttps://theprint.in/india/yogi-govt-completes-skill-mapping-of-23-5-lakh-migrant-workers-18-lakh-want-jobs-in-up/435450/.
3. Seehttps://indianexpress.com/article/explained/uttar-pradesh-migrant-labourers-mnrega-job-employment-coronavirus-6476830/.
4. Seehttps://www.business-standard.com/article/economy-policy/fm-allocates-rs-40-000-crore-more-for-mgnrega-to-support-migrants-120051701175_1.html.
5. Seehttps://indianexpress.com/article/explained/uttar-pradesh-migrant-labourers-mnrega-job-employment-coronavirus-6476830/.
6. Seehttp://mnregaweb4.nic.in/netnrega/MISreport4.aspx.
7. Seehttp://mnregaweb4.nic.in/netnrega/MISreport4.aspx.
8. Seehttps://www.hindustantimes.com/india-news/3-5-million-new-enrolments-under-mgnrega-as-distressed-workers-return-to-villages/story-aDJHYz0vz1tSeLleIhVT7I.html.

9. http://mnregaweb4.nic.in/netnrega/MISreport4.aspx
10. Seehttps://indianexpress.com/article/india/first-time-panchayat-funds-to-be-audited-online-6522285/.
11. Seehttp://socialauditup.in/gos.php.
12. https://www.jagran.com/bihar/begusarai-social-audit-and-public-hearing-program-organized-in-pahasara-19827880.html
13. Ashish Ranjan and Puroshottam Kumar, A New Twist to Social Audits, http://www.indiatogether.org/audit-poverty
14. Page 3, Audit Standards for Social Audit, Ministry of Rural Development, Government of India.
15. Page 4, Ibid.
16. Ibid.
17. Audit Standards for Social Audit, Ministry of Rural Development, Government of India.
18. All villages to be connected with optical fiber in next 1000 days, https://timesofindia.indiatimes.com/business/india-business/all-villages-to-be-connected-with-optical-fibre-in-next-1000-days-pm-modi/articleshow/77558650.cms

Index

A

Aajeevika Farm Fresh, 128
Absence of work, 33
Academic Loss, 149
Aches and pains, 13
Adam Smith, 113
Aga Khan Rural Support Programme, 17
Agricultural laborer, 137, 140
Agriculture and Allied Sectors, 136
Agriculture and Rural Development, 64
Airtel, 165
Alkem Laboratory, 163
Amitava Gupta, 108
Amrita News Service, 16
Ananda Bazar Patrika, 108
Anchalik Panchayat, 76
Ancillary nurse mid-wives, 64
Andhra Pradesh, 52, 55, 56, 130, 131, 159
Anganwadi workers, 88, 90
Annual Status of Education Report, 146
Antodaya Anna Yojana, 47
Arogya Setu, 160
Artisan-entrepreneur, 120
Arunachal Pradesh, 75
Asanbani, 64
Assam, 120
Assam Panchayat Act, 76
Assam-Gaon Panchayat, 76
Assessment of Impact to Draw Future Lessons, 153
Atmanirbhar Bharat, 18
Audio Visual, 130
Audit Online, 171
Awareness Campaigns, 78

B

Baba Saheb Ambedkar Hastshilp Vikash Yojana, 117
Bahrain, 51
Bandipora, 46
Bangladesh, 51
Bank is far away, 45
Bank Linkage Program, 65
Bapuji Handloom Weavers' Co-operative Society, 138, 141
Barka Gaon village, 148
Basic essential items, 46
Begusarai, 172
Bihar, 15, 20, 25, 52, 55, 95, 127, 159, 172
Bleaching powder, 45
Brahmaputra River, 75
Brand Mantra, 120
Building and Construction Workers, 37
Burtuk, 161

C

Cash flow constraint, 105
Cash liquidity, 121
Cash Transfer, 108
Central Pendam, 161
Challenges in Agricultural Sector, 104
Chanatar, 161
Cherai Handloom Weavers Co-operative Society, 120

Chhattisgarh, 44, 68, 131
Child abuse, 42
China, 14, 133
Chronic medical conditions, 13
City to rural areas, 35
Civil Society Organisations, 18, 48, 69
Civil society organisations, 42, 126
Cluster Development Program, 117
Cluster Federation level, 128
Collaboration with Private Sector, 154
Communication Campaigns and Information Sharing, 153
Community Disaster Response Force, 92
Community Health Centers, 15
Community Kitchen, 69
Compensatory Afforestation Management, 18
Compulsory lockdown, 30
Construction workers, 163
Containment zone, 107
Corona positive cases, 77
Corona Virus, 14
Corona Virus disease, 85
Cottage and small industries, 16
Craftsmen and artisans, 49
Cultural and social differences, 43
Curfew and Lockdown, 142
Cyclone, 74

D

Dahod, 16
Daily sanitization, 18
Debt Traps, 35
Decrease farm wages, 35
Deendayal Antyodaya Yojana, 125, 126
Delhi, 159
Deorali, 161
Department of Rural development, 175
Deserted Women Pension, 49
Design Centre, 120
Dharmendra Pradhan, 64
Dhenkanal district, 64
Diarrhoea, 13
Didi helpline, 128
Digital Technology, 152
Direct Implementation projects, 43
Disabled farmers, 49
Disaster Management Act, 21
Disaster Management Committees, 81
Disaster Mitigation plan, 91
Disinfectants and masks, 47
Disrupted education, 149
Distribution of essential supplies, 47
Distribution of Financial Assistance, 81
Distribution of free food grains, 22
District administration, 18, 129
District Collector, 22, 89
District Disaster Management Authority, 22, 76, 86
District Programme Coordinator, 97
Domestic worker, 44
Dry cough, 13

E

E-Pathshala, 152
Earthquake, 74
Economic Health, 104
Economic Impact of Lockdown, 135
Education health and marital status, 99
Education sector, 148
Effect on Children and their Education, 106
Effect on Women, 106
Epidemic Diseases Act, 14
Essential food supplies, 47
Exogenous factor, 106
Expanding Edutech Platforms Amidst Lockdown, 152

F

Farmers and manual labourers, 22
Farming Produce Trade, 109

Farming Produce Trade and Commerce, 109
Fertilizer shortage, 105
Financial difficulties, 48
Financial problem, 47
Foreign workers, 51, 55
Friendly food parks, 37

G

Gaon Connection survey, 148
Garib Kalyan Yojana, 108
Gas cylinder, 45
Gender inequalities, 41
Gender-based violence, 42
Global financial crisis, 58
Global Hunger Index, 104
Government facility, 45
Government of Telangana, 24, 140, 141
GP level disaster management committees, 82
Gram Panchayat, 18, 25, 70, 74, 87, 90, 101, 169
Gram Panchayat areas, 89
Gram Panchayat Bhawan, 173
Gram Panchayat Development Plan, 111
Grameen Sahara, 17
Green Tea, 47
Green vegetables, 80
Grocery items, 46
Growth of agro-based industries, 37
Gruhalaxmi Cooperative Self Help Group, 64
Guaranteed Emergency Credit Line, 18, 109
Gujarat, 15, 68, 96
Gulf companies, 56
Gulf Cooperation Council, 51
Gulf countries, 51, 54, 55, 57, 58, 60
Gulf migrant workers, 57
Gulf migration, 60
Gulf region, 57, 60
Gulf War, 52

H

Hand sanitizers, 129
Handicraft cluster, 119, 122
Handicraft clusters of India, 117
Handicraft industry, 23
Haryana, 68
Hasuri Ausanpur village, 150
Health sector, 25
Health workers, 25
Himachal Pradesh, 66, 130
Hindol block, 64
Hong Kong, 14
Huzurabad, 135, 138
Huzurabad Mandal, 134

I

Ice cream vendor, 138
ICT Status in Rural India, 147
Impact of Lockdown, 135
Implementation of MGNREGA, 22
Imran Kasim, 120
Indian Embassies, 59
Indian Express, 31
Indian handicraft sector, 118
Indo Asian News Service, 119
Indo Global Social Service Society, 42
Industrial Infrastructure Up gradation Scheme, 117
Internal migration, 31
International demand, 23
International migration, 31
Internet and Mobile Association of India, 148
Interrupted supply chain, 121
Iraq-Kuwait war, 52
Isolation ward, 160

J

Jammikunta, 135
Jammu and Kashmir, 35, 46

Jammu and Kashmir Rural Livelihood Mission, 128
Jan-Dhan scheme, 45
Jharkhand, 15, 34, 66, 95, 130
Jio, 165
Job under MGNREGA, 22

K

K. Sadanandam, 138
Kandhamal, 46
Karimnagar District, 134
Karl Marx, 113
Karnataka, 66, 159
Kashmir Rural Livelihoods Mission, 23
Kenya, 145
Kerala, 20, 52, 55, 56, 68, 75, 127, 130, 159
Khadi Gramudyog, 127
Khidmat Centre, 47
Kisan Samman Nidhi scheme, 18
Kisan Yojana, 108
Kudumbashree network, 127
Kurunti Nuagaon, 64
Kuwait, 51

L

Labour unavailability, 105
Less investment in handicraft products, 121
Livelihood opportunities, 99
Livestock rearers, 49
Local authorities, 45
Local communities, 93
Local governance, 93
Local Government, 49, 86
Local leaders, 93
Local organisations, 93
Local Self Government, 86
Local volunteers, 88
Lockdown time, 33
Loss of livelihood, 48
LPG gas, 45

M

Madhya Pradesh, 15, 66, 68, 95, 109, 130, 131
Maharashtra, 15, 44, 95, 131, 159
Mahatma Gandhi, 73, 97, 113
Management Information System, 97
Marginalized sections, 42
Masks and Sanitizers, 77
Medical quarantine, 160
Medicines without prescriptions, 45
MGNREGA, 96, 169
MGNREGA details, 173
Micro, Small and Medium Enterprises, 18, 109
Migrant labour, 30, 98
Migrant workers, 57, 80
Migration of Labor, 121
Migration to Gulf, 52
Mission Shakti, 64
Mizoram, 66, 130, 131
Modernise agriculture markets, 37
Monetary Policy Committee, 112
Most Backward Caste, 162
MSME Clusters, 115
Muhammad Yunus, 109
Muhkya Mantri Didi Kitchen, 128
Multimedia communications, 172
Mumbai, 159
Municipal corporations, 15
Mustered oil, 47
Muzaffarpur, 148

N

Nagaland, 66, 120, 131
Nagaon district, 75
Namchi, 161
Narendrapur, 64
National Bank, 64
National Bank for Agriculture and Rural Developmen, 17, 65
National challenge, 85

National Disaster Management, 14
National Disaster Management Act, 104
National Disaster Mitigation Plan, 91
National Disaster Response Force, 91
National Food Security Card, 89
National Mission Management Unit, 128
National Panchayati Raj Day, 75
National Rural Employment Guarantee Act, 22
National Rural Livelihood Mission, 67, 125, 126
Natural Resource Management, 97, 169
Naveen Pattnaik, 64
Nepal, 51
New York Times, 34, 35
Nobel laureate, 109
Nobel laureate Abhijit Binayak Banerjee, 110
Non Performing Assets, 67
Non-Agriculture Sectors, 138
Non-farm employment opportunities, 37
Non-payment of rent, 49
North Eastern states, 68

O

Odisha, 15, 34, 46, 75, 96
Odiya Basti, 44
Oman, 51
On food production, 105
Other Backward Caste, 162
Own Source Revenues, 89

P

Padmashali Officials and Professionals Association, 141
Pahsarapurvi panchayat, 172
Pakistan, 51
Panchayat Disaster Mitigation Plan, 91
Panchayati Raj, 73, 171
Panchayati Raj Institutions, 17, 21, 74, 86, 90, 97, 126
Panchayati Raj system, 73, 76, 111
Panchayats Level Disaster Management, 81
Panchayat's work, 46
Pandemic and lockdown, 19, 41, 44
Pandemic strategy, 75
Payment of wages, 100
Payment of wages and salaries, 54
Pension cards, 45
Permanent disaster management committee, 82
Pharmaceutical employees, 163
Philippines, 51
Physical verification of assets, 174
Policy and Institutional Responses, 151
Poor households, 129
Portability of ration cards, 37
Postponement of Marriages, 139
Pradhan Mantri Garib Kalyan Yojana, 36, 141
President Sabita Nayak, 64
Preventive Actions, 152
Primary Health Care, 46
Primary Health Centers, 15, 166
Primary Skill Building, 92
Prime Minister Kisan Yojana, 17
Prime Minister Narendra Modi, 30, 75
Prime Minister's Garib Kalyan Package, 17
Prioritisation of health infrastructure, 37
Private hospital, 45
Private Limited Companies, 117
Problem of distribution, 106
Problem of selling, 106
Processing facility, 37
Prof. Amartya Sen, 87
Programme Officer, 97
Pronab Sen, 107
Public Distribution System, 89, 108
Public Health, 104
Public health measures, 14
Puducherry, 66

Punjab, 35, 52, 55, 109
Purchasing Power Parity, 104

Q

Qatar, 51
Quality Educations, 147
Quarantine centres, 77
Quarantined people, 81

R

Rabi crop, 104
Raipur, 44
Rajasthan, 35, 52, 55, 56, 66
Rampur, 141
Rampur village, 134
Ranipool, 161
Ration card, 77
Rented accommodation, 49
Resilient Reopening of Schools, 153
Restriction on the movement, 46
Retail outlet, 37
Reverse migration, 35
Review and documentary analysis, 174
Rice, 47
Right to Education, 146
Rongli, 161
Runny nose, 13
Rural and urban areas, 38
Rural Economy, 104
Rural economy and livelihoods, 24
Rural Education, 18, 147
Rural Education and Challenges, 148
Rural Education in India, 24, 146
Rural health, 18
Rural India, 15, 122
Rural infrastructure, 18
Rural Livelihoods, 24, 135, 139
Rural Local Governments, 86
Rural migrants, 30, 37
Rural People, 135
Rural Raipur, 44
Rural society of Sikkim, 25
Rural wage employment, 22
Rural women, 48
Rural-urban migration, 110

S

Sanitary napkins, 45
Sanitation essentials, 46
Sanitization, 79
Sanitization programme, 79
Sarva Shiksha Abhiyan scheme, 149
Saudi Arabia, 51
School education institutions, 156
School management, 140
Self Help Group, 23, 63, 65, 88, 125, 130
Self-Help Promoting Institutions, 65
Semi-urban centres, 96
Serious public health pandemic, 71
Severe Acute Respiratory Syndrome, 13
Shalini James, 120
Sharda Gautam, 120
SHG development, 66
Shutdown of production, 22
Sikkim, 66
Sikkim's Health and Family Welfare Department, 160
Single woman, 42, 43, 44, 45, 48, 49
Singtam, 161
Skilling of rural youth, 18
Snowball sampling, 43
Social audit, 172
Social Audit of MGNREGA, 170
Social distancing, 33
Sonitpur, 77, 79
Sonitpur district, 75
Sore throat, 13
South Asian countries, 51
Sri Lanka, 51
State Disaster Mitigation Plan, 91
State Disaster Response Force, 92
State Governments, 18

State Rural Livelihood Mission, 127, 128
State Rural Livelihoods Missions, 130
Statistician of India, 107
Stove to cook rice, 45
Stranded workers, 57
Sujata R. Karthikeyan, 64
Sumerdung, 161
Summer vacation, 140
Support to Family Income, 154
Surendranagar, 16
Sustainable Development Goals, 24, 111

T

Tamil Nadu, 20, 52, 55, 56, 65, 66, 130, 131, 159
Tata Trusts, 120
Taxi drivers, 163
Technology Driven Education with Equity, 152
Technology Driven Online Education, 153
Telangana, 15, 52, 55, 56, 95
Telangana Poultry Association, 136
The rural areas of Assam, 82
Timburbung, 161
Togo, 145
Traditional Industries, 117
Transform Rural India Foundation, 17
Transgender communities, 41
Transportation facilities, 48
Transportation to supply production, 23
Travel sectors, 51
Tripura, 66

U

Ujjwala card, 46
UN Policy Brief, 147
Unavailability of vehicles, 46, 49
Uncertain future, 16
Unemployment, 55
UNESCO, 159
United Nation, 165, 163
Unlimited Supply of Labour, 110
Unmarried teacher, 140
Unorganized sector's workers, 105
Upgrade food processing clusters, 37
Urban areas, 99
Urban landscape, 43
Urban middle-class single women, 43
Urban middle-class women, 41
Use of education resources, 153
Using handkerchiefs, 45
Uttar Pradesh, 15, 20, 25, 34, 52, 55, 56, 68, 95, 109, 127, 169, 172
Uttarakhand, 35, 66, 109

V

Varanasi, 120
Village Councils, 97
Village Defence Force, 77
Village Defence Police, 21, 81
Violence against women, 42
Virus causing infection, 29
Vodafone, 165

W

West Asia, 51
West Bengal, 15, 35, 55, 74, 117
Widow pension, 46, 49
Women empowerment, 64
Women SHGs, 18
Women-elected representatives, 174
World Bank, 18, 31, 32
World Bank report, 55
World Health Organization, 13, 29, 33, 85, 95, 103, 126, 131
Worldwide pandemic, 29
Wuhan city, 133

Z

Zilla Parishad, 76
Zimbabwe, 145
Zitlang, 161
Zoom or Webex, 148